General editor: Graham Handley MA Ph.D.

Brodie's Notes on Virginia Woolf's
To the Lighthouse

Perdita V. Hooper BA

MACMILLAN

First published 1979 by Pan Books Ltd

This revised edition published 1993 by
THE MACMILLAN PRESS LTD
Houndmills, Basingstoke, Hampshire RG21 2XS
and London
Companies and representatives
throughout the world

ISBN 0–333–60930–1

Typeset by Footnote Graphics, Warminster, Wiltshire
Printed in Great Britain by
Cox & Wyman Ltd, Reading

Contents

Preface

The intention throughout this study aid is to stimulate and guide, to encourage your involvement in the book, and to develop informed responses and a sure understanding of the main details.

Brodie's Notes provide a clear outline of the play or novel's plot, followed by act, scene, or chapter summaries and/or commentaries. These are designed to emphasize the most important literary and factual details. Poems, stories or non-fiction texts combine brief summary with critical commentary on individual aspects or common features of the genre being examined. Textual notes define what is difficult or obscure and emphasize literary qualities. Revision questions are set at appropriate points to test your ability to appreciate the prescribed book and to write accurately and relevantly about it.

In addition, each of these Notes includes a critical appreciation of the author's art. This covers such major elements as characterization, style, structure, setting and themes. Poems are examined technically – rhyme, rhythm, for instance. In fact, any important aspect of the prescribed work will be evaluated. The aim is to send you back to the text you are studying.

Each study aid concludes with a series of general questions which require a detailed knowledge of the book: some of these questions may invite comparison with other books, some will be suitable for coursework exercises, and some could be adapted to work you are doing on another book or books. Each study aid has been adapted to meet the needs of the current examination requirements. They provide a basic, individual and imaginative response to the work being studied, and it is hoped that they will stimulate you to acquire disciplined reading habits and critical fluency.

Graham Handley 1990

A close reading of the set book is the student's primary task. These Notes will help to increase your understanding and appreciation of the novel, and to stimulate *your own* thinking about it; *they are in no way intended as a substitute* for a thorough knowledge of the book.

References are given to individual Parts and Sections so that the Notes may be used with any edition of the novel.

The author and her work

Virginia Stephen was born in 1882, the third child of Leslie Stephen's marriage to Julia Duckworth, who already had three older children from a previous marriage – George, Stella and Gerald. It was Virginia's father's second marriage too, and he was fifty when she was born. Stephen was a stern, moral, highly intellectual man, who had given up his fellowship at Cambridge for reasons of conscience, and had come to London to work as a journalist and writer. He was interested in philosophy and literary criticism, fiercely committed to radical politics, and had begun work on *The Dictionary of National Biography*, which was to prove arduous and taxing.

Virginia's mother, noted for her beauty, came from an artistic family; she was playful and light-hearted with her children, while having to fortify, protect and support the morale of her husband, who worried over his work, his reputation and financial matters. Husband and wife were deeply in love: she living for him, soothing him and easing domestic burdens; while he much appreciated her goodness and serenity. The children Thoby, Vanessa, Virginia and Adrian were a very close-knit family, all sleeping in the nursery at the top of the house in Hyde Park Gate, providing themselves with their own entertainment and even producing their own newspaper. The deep attachment between Vanessa and Virginia was to last all their lives. As a child, Virginia seemed rather eccentric: prone to accidents, unpredictable and highly sensitive to criticism; she was nicknamed 'the goat' by the family after various escapades. In 1888 she had whooping-cough badly, took a long time to recover, and her health was ever after to remain fragile. Some of the happiest childhood times were the summer holidays spent at Talland House in St Ives, Cornwall, where they were free to go for long walks, visit the lighthouse, sail, fish and play in the garden; and where there was always a large company of visiting family friends. Virginia remembered those summer months as an idyllic time.

Vanessa and Virginia were educated at home, their father not being really modern enough to consider that they needed to go to school and university as their brothers did. They had governesses, were read to in the evenings by their father (Sir Walter Scott was one of his favourite novelists), and encouraged to read widely themselves. Virginia appreciated the freedom that she was given over books, an unusual privilege in those Victorian times.

Her mother, probably overworked and over anxious, died in 1895. 'Her death was the greatest disaster that could happen,' wrote Virginia later, and it had far-reaching effects on the household. Leslie Stephen, ridden with guilt, abandoned himself entirely to grief, and the family atmosphere became dark and oppressive. He dominated his family, crushing them with the demands of his unrelenting egotism. It was then that Virginia had her first breakdown. She became very nervous and excitable, felt depressed, thought she heard voices, and was terrified of meeting people. And her pulse raced, while at the same time she suffered a complete loss of appetite. She recovered slowly, but these symptoms were to recur and to become worse in later years.

In time, Thoby and Adrian went to Cambridge where they had a large circle of friends, many of whom were afterwards to form the nucleus of what became known as the 'Bloomsbury Group'. Virginia was always envious of this intellectual, masculine world and the freedom that it offered. Vanessa was able to escape from family pressures by her interest in art; she went to the Royal Academy School, but she herself felt very much restrained by her father.

In 1904 Sir Leslie Stephen died, and though in a sense this was a release, and enabled Virginia to begin to write, she had terrible guilt feelings and became increasingly nervous and irritable. A holiday in Florence with Vanessa, who was delighted to be free, was unsatisfactory, and Virginia returned to London, where she had her second breakdown – this one verging on madness. She tried to commit suicide by throwing herself from a window. Once again she recovered, but in 1905 began writing articles for *The Times Literary Supplement*, work which she continued to do all her life.

In that same year the Stephen family decided to leave the atmosphere of the old family house and moved to Gordon Square, Bloomsbury. Here they found the liberty they sought, and the Cambridge friends of Thoby were frequent visitors. The Bloomsbury Group consisted of intellectual and artistic people, many of whom had been influential at Cambridge and were quite brilliant in their individual spheres. There was the painter, poet, musician Saxon Sydney-Turner; the art critic Clive Bell; the artist Roger Fry; the historian and writer Lytton Strachey, later to produce *Eminent Victorians* (1918); the economist Maynard Keynes; the writer E. M. Forster. There were also Walter Lamb, Desmond McCarthy, Leonard Woolf and, later, the artist Duncan Grant, as well as many others who came and went. They were united by a feeling of conscious revolt against Victorian values and habits, of thinking that still lingered on. They demanded freedom and truth, particularly sexual freedom, and they shocked the outside world by their relationships, their openness, their unconventionality.

Virginia revelled in this atmosphere, though she continued to have bouts of illness. She was experimenting, writing what was to become *The Voyage Out* (published 1915), but she set herself such high standards that she was frequently depressed. During these years she had several offers of marriage, none of which she could take seriously; and her deepest affections had until now been given to her great friend, Violet Dickinson. But gradually this friendship cooled and finally, in 1912, after much doubt, depression, hesitation and feelings of inadequacy, she agreed to marry Leonard Woolf, himself a writer, who had spent much time in Ceylon as a colonial administrator.

This marriage was to develop into a deeply loving relationship, with Virginia becoming more and more dependent on her husband's support. She always found writing an exhausting process, but once the books were finished she went through anguish, waiting to discover what the reactions to them would be. She was morbidly hypersensitive to criticism, and Leonard had always to try to convince her of the worth of her writing. She had a major breakdown in 1913 while waiting for the publication of *The Voyage Out*, once again trying to commit suicide, this time through an overdose of veronal. She recovered somewhat, after the largely favourable reviews, and began to work on her next book, which was eventually to become *Night and Day* (1919). She also kept a journal, which was published by her husband in 1953 as *A Writer's Diary*. In 1917 the Woolfs bought a printing-press and began to issue their own works. The Hogarth Press, despite early financial and management difficulties, was to prove extremely successful over the years, producing all Virginia's works; also books by T. S. Eliot, Katherine Mansfield, John Middleton Murry, E. M. Forster and Maxim Gorky. The Woolfs were even offered James Joyce's *Ulysses*, but felt at the time that they could not cope with it. Later, in the 1930s, the Hogarth Press became associated with left-wing writers such as Stephen Spender, C. Day Lewis, W. H. Auden and Christopher Isherwood.

With the publication of *Jacob's Room* in 1922 – and this was well received – came the beginning of Virginia Woolf's fame. She was now well established as a writer, the Press was going well and she enjoyed working there, sometimes setting type, sometimes acting as a packer. Her social life was increasing, for the Bloomsbury Group continued to provide her with intellectual stimulus. She could be gay and witty, quick to laughter, enjoying the friendship of people she respected.

Mrs Dalloway was finished in 1924, and, though she was ill again in 1925, the period that followed was largely one of great achievement: she published *To the Lighthouse* in 1927, and *The Waves* in 1931. It was also the time of her close friendship with Vita Sackville-West, and the lighthearted *Orlando* published in 1928, celebrates Vita and the Sackville-West family. In 1930, when she had finished *The Waves*, Virginia entered in her diary that she felt she had 'netted that fin in the waste of water which appeared to me over the marshes at Rodmell when I was coming to an end of *To the Lighthouse*'. This 'fin in the water' seems to be a symbol of her anxiety, her depression, her fear of failure.

Flush (1933), the fictional biography of Elizabeth Barrett Browning's dog, coming between *The Waves* and *The Years*, seems to have provided an escape for Virginia, just as *Orlando* had done earlier, for it was less demanding, less taxing on her nerves. She found the writing of *The Years*, published in 1937, extraordinarily difficult. No one else seemed to be writing in that style; the literary revolution had not taken place; she seemed alone. She was baffled and anxious, writing and re-writing: by his praise of the book Leonard Woolf probably saved her life, so depressed and increasingly uncertain had she become.

The next few years were difficult. The coming of war seemed to bring ruin. The Woolfs were now quite wealthy, but Leonard was a Jew and a socialist, and husband and wife comtemplated suicide in the event of the Germans winning. The world seemed unstable: friends had died or been killed; life in London was impossible. Virginia finished *Between the Acts* in February 1941, but she was so depressed that she did not want it published. Her health deteriorated, and she became critically ill. On 28 March 1941 she wrote two letters, one to her husband and one to her sister, telling them that her old symptoms was recurring, and that she could fight them no longer. Then she left the house and drowned herself in the River Ouse.

Virginia Woolf felt that if her father had not died, she would have been unable to write novels, so constrained was her life. But she did have a deep love and respect for him too which caused her great feelings of guilt, and another breakdown, after his death. She needed to get him out of her system, as she herself realized, and *To the Lighthouse* contains in a sense, two portraits: one of her father and one of her mother. Her sister Vanessa was impressed by Mrs Ramsay: she thought the picture was a good likeness of their mother.

In *To the Lighthouse* the author has used many incidents and people from her own life. The setting is reminiscent of their holiday home at St Ives: the garden, the beach, the lighthouse are all there; and the season is the happy one of summer. Among their visitors at St Ives had been a man who took opium and a girl who became engaged while she was there. Virigina's elder brother Thoby died very young, her step-sister died in childbirth, and her own mother when Virginia was only thirteen. There is an incident in her writing as a child where she tells of the occasion when her young brother, Adrian, was very disappointed at not going on a trip to the lighthouse: Virginia always felt that she and Adrian were thwarted and repressed by their father.

Virginia's mother was admired for her beauty, and was something of a matchmaker; her father was fond of Sir Walter Scott, liked reciting poetry aloud, and could never restrain his feelings. These and many other details make the Ramsays obvious portraits of the Stephens; but Virginia Woolf was an artist, and she refashioned and worked upon the material of her own experience. Thus the Ramsays, far more than being mere replicas of her parents, blend into the schematic structure of the novel.

The writer and the form of the novel

In the years between the wars there were many writers who felt dissatisfied with the form of the conventional novel, its treatment of a span of time, its plot, its rounded characters, its single viewpoint. In France, influenced by Henri Bergson, Proust had already experimented with time-shifts and changing perceptions of external reality in *À la Recherche du temps perdu* (1913), while in English novelists as different as Henry James and D. H. Lawrence had shown increasing interest and awareness of the psychology of character, what was happening in the mind rather than in momentous and exciting events. They concentrated on the significance of relatively trivial or mundane things which are made interesting by the reactions of the characters to them.

In England Dorothy Richardson pioneered the type of novel that was to be called 'stream of consciousness' in her twelve-part sequence *Pilgrimage*, written between 1915 and 1938. And in *Ulysses* (1922) James Joyce produced a huge novel dealing with the events of just one day in Dublin. The 'stream of consciousness' method was an attempt to portray life as it really is, through the perceptions of a character as each event occurs. Many of the writers of the period were experimenting, using different time strata as their characters' memories operated, and basing novels on relatively short periods of time – in an attempt to capture 'real life' more completely. With a very short time span, great exterior changes do not happen: there are only the ordinary or mundane happenings of normal life, so that the interest switches to the interior changes occurring in the characters' minds. The continuity of the novel then lies in the minds of the people, and external events are only presented as being important if they encroach upon the consciousness of the character. A natural progression from dealing with the mind of one person is to deal with several, and many of the novels of the time have this many-faceted viewpoint in their interior monologues.

Virginia Woolf did not find the conventional novel satisfactory either; she was particularly critical of the work of her immediate predecessors, Arnold Bennett, H. G. Wells and John Galsworthy. In her essay 'Mr Bennett and Mrs Brown', she attacks them for being materialists, more interested in people's social welfare and conditions than in their minds. She admits that they deal with life, but for her it is not the 'real' life of the inner spirit or mind. She feels that the traditional elements of the novel – plot, love, tragedy, comedy, with all the strands tied up at the end – impose an unnatural strain on the author. Life is complex, untidy, difficult to grasp; it should not be summed up so neatly. In making this assertion she is in part influenced by her friend E. M. Forster, and later by his study *Aspects of the Novel* (1927).

In an essay on 'Modern Fiction' Virginia Woolf examines the marvellous complexity of what she calls the 'ordinary mind', but in her novels she explores the intelligent or artistic mind, which is even more aware and intricate. In this essay she also tells us what she feels should be the main concerns of the novel: it should give a sense of reality, of what life is like; of the compound perceptions haphazardly gained, and of people's attempts to make something of these perceptions. She believes that 'Life is not a series of gig-lamps symmetrically arranged; life is a luminous halo, a semi-transparent envelope surrounding us from the beginning of consciousness to the end.'

So Virginia Woolf experimented with a new form. In the case of *To the Lighthouse*, she was not even sure it could be called a novel, and wondered if 'elegy' were not more appropriate. However, though she often used the 'stream of consciousness' method in her interior monologues, she was aware of the dangers of this technique, realizing that the writing could become pointless and amorphous. The writer must select, control and fashion his work into some kind of shape and synthesis. The author must present to the reader something distilled, clear and whole. The reader will note how she practised what she preached in terms of structure and control in *To the Lighthouse*.

Plot and structure

Plot

It is difficult, when outlining the plot of *To the Light-house*, to give a clear-cut synopsis of the story. The author herself, as we have just seen, wondered whether it should be called an 'elegy' rather than a novel. The book might also be compared to a symphony – in which there are separate 'movements', but with themes that recur several times throughout, variously elaborated, and interpreted by different 'instruments'.

In Part 1, 'The Window', Mrs Ramsay is sitting at the window of their holiday home on a Scottish island, early one September evening, knitting and talking to James, her youngest child. In the garden, Mr Ramsay and Charles Tansley are walking together on the terrace; and Lily Briscoe is on the lawn painting a picture of the house and garden, showing Mrs Ramsay at the window. Mr Carmichael is sitting alone outside; Cam is playing; Jasper is shooting birds; and William Dankes joins Lily and talks to her. Minta Doyle, Paul Rayley, Andrew and Nancy Ramsay have gone to the beach.

As the people in the garden walk about, they are seen by Mrs Ramsay, and this triggers off her thoughts about them; and, as they see her in the window, they also think about her. Mr Ramsay and Mr Tansley stop on the terrace to tell James and Mrs Ramsay that the weather will be too bad for them to go to the Lighthouse next day. Mr Tansley then goes off to continue work on his dissertation, and Mr Ramsay goes on pacing the terrace, reciting poetry to himself, considering philosophical problems and stopping occasionally at the window to speak to his wife.

William Bankes and Lily stroll in the garden talking of Mr Ramsay, of art, and both thinking about Mrs Ramsay. The latter has herself been angered by the dashing of James's hopes of going to the Lighthouse. Her thoughts wander over Tansley, Lily Briscoe, her children, the Swiss maid, Augustus Carmichael and her husband. She tells James a story and worries about the safety of the beach party who have not yet returned.

After James has gone to bed, Mr and Mrs Ramsay walk through the garden together, talking and watching the play of Jasper and Prue. When she dresses for dinner, helped by the children, Rose and Jasper, Mrs Ramsay hears the others return from the beach. Paul and Minta have become engaged, but Minta is upset about losing her brooch.

At dinner that night family and visitors come together, though Paul and Minta are late. Boeuf en Daube, a special dish, has been cooked for the occasion because William Bankes has agreed to stay. Although there is tension and a feeling of irritation among the diners at first, later – with the arrival of the lovers – everyone becomes happier and more relaxed. The dinner party is a success.

After dinner, Mrs Ramsay tends to the needs of Cam and James, the two youngest, and returns to her husband. They sit together, reading, enjoying each other's company, aware of each other's love.

In Part 2, 'Time Passes', the darkness and passing of one night merge into the darkness of many nights – ten years, in fact. With the passing of time comes tragedy: the death of Mrs Ramsay; the death of Prue in childbirth; the death of Andrew in war. As the years go past, the house in Scotland is ravaged by the processes of time, and Mrs McNab, the charwoman, desperately fights a losing battle to keep it in order. But at last, when the war is over, the family return and the two charwomen restore the house as much as possible. Lily Briscoe and Augustus Carmichael, whose volume of poems has been a great success, are again visitors.

In Part 3, The Lighthouse', the interest has two centres. Lily returns to painting her picture, which she had never finished. As she paints, her mind hovers over the people she knows; events she has experienced; trying to piece things together. She concentrates on Mrs Ramsay, whom she misses, at the same time being fascinated by Mr Ramsay and his expedition to the Lighthouse. At the end, she finishes her picture, knowing that the expedition has reached its goal, and having had a kind of vision of the meaning of Mrs Ramsay.

Meanwhile, Mr Ramsay is taking the reluctant Cam and James to the Lighthouse. They resent his overbearing manner, but gradually their resistance to him is worn down, and they join in his excitement at the prospect of reaching their destination. They follow him on to the rock
gladly; the expedition has succeeded at the same time as Lily's picture has reached completion.

Structure

The basic framework of the novel is chronological, though individual characters are taken back in time by their thoughts. The novel is divided into three parts; there are no chapters, but each Part is divided into numbered Sections. Part 1 (by far the longest Part), deals with the mundane happenings of one afternoon and evening. Part 2 is the night, which is extended to ten years of darkness. Part 3 takes in just one morning –

when the journey to the Lighthouse, and Lily's paintings, are finally completed.

Just as one of Virginia Woolf's main themes is time and the effects of time, so the form of the book too reflects it. She seems to expand time in the first section, with long descriptive passages of a character's thoughts between a question and an answer. The direct speech of the moment is desultory and brief, sandwiched between long, contemplative, slow-moving interior monologues. The first part 'The Window', is largely static, the main characters moving gently round Mrs Ramsay, who is first of all at the window, then presiding at dinner. It is exploratory in nature, touching on relationships and personalities, centring on Mrs Ramsay but introducing Lily's picture and the idea of going to the Lighthouse.

The second part 'The Passing of Time', has ten sections in which ten years go by. This part is highly poetic, concentrating on the forces of time, darkness and chaos – where people are distanced, made small and unimportant, their deaths being passed over briefly. This is the shortest part, but the fact that ten years pass underlines man's predicament in the vastness of eternity. This section seems to stand back in order to assess man's position, as opposed to the first part where the minutiae of people's thoughts and feelings are given.

The third part has more movement than the first, though fewer characters; there is more sense of purpose in the two linked events. The double climax of the book gives a sense of completeness and of satisfaction, rather as did the dinner-party in the first section. The time scheme here is complicated, dealing with two contemporaneous happenings in which people face their memories and use them constructively. The past lives on in the future. All three sections are linked by the island setting, the Lighthouse, and the character of Mrs Ramsay, who lives on in other minds.

Although the book gives the thoughts of many different people, the structure is highly controlled. The links between events and reactions are neatly done. Mr Ramsay, declaiming 'someone had blundered', bears down on Lily and William Bankes. This leads to their thinking about Mr Ramsay and discussing him. Images 'exploded' in Lily's mind at the same time as Jasper's shot goes off. Following the fleeing birds, the two step straight into Mr Ramsay and his 'someone had blundered'. The irony is enjoyable. The association of thoughts, events and people is emphasized by obvious links, and there is never a muddle. By her use of numbered sections, Virginia Woolf keeps her main characters separate. We know what is happening indoors, in the garden, what takes place on the lawn, or at sea; the structure is tight, coherent, skilfully controlled.

Section summaries, critical commentary, textual notes and revision questions

Part 1 The Window

Section 1

Mrs Ramsay is sitting at the window of the holiday house in the Hebrides with her small son James. She promises him that they will visit the Lighthouse next day if it is fine. James is filled with expectancy and joy at this, but is crushed the next moment by his father appearing at the window and telling them that it would not be fine. Note the different attitudes of Mr and Mrs Ramsay: she wishes to encourage the little boy, and he, 'incapable of untruth, never tampered with a fact', forces his son to face the unpleasant truth. Note also the way in which the short dialogue is interspersed with long passages of description as characters' inner feelings, lines of thought and reactions are revealed.

Charles Tansley, a visitor and disciple of Mr Ramsay, agrees with him about the weather – which leads to Mrs Ramsay's thoughts about him; her children's reactions to him; their holiday visitors; the male sex in general; and then marriage. As Tansely speaks again, so she remembers her children's criticisms of him. He is a dry academic, proud to have the friendship of Mr Ramsay, socially awkward and completely egocentric. Logically, Mrs Ramsay's thoughts take her back a few days.

The meal over, her children retire to their rooms; Tansley is left alone. Mrs Ramsay ponders on the difficulties and stresses of relationships and is irritated by them, seeing the greater problems of poverty as more real and important, yet insoluble. She makes an effort, however, to be kind to Charles Tansley (who has been deserted by everyone else) and suggests that he should accompany her to the town. On their way out they pass Mr Carmichael, basking in the sunshine, and Mrs Ramsay talks to Tansley of his failure to be a great philosopher (because of his marriage), of his resort to drug-taking, and his generally passive approach to life.

As Mrs Ramsay talks to him Charles Tansley revives, feels less awkward and becomes more expansive and self-assured, but he is unable to share her excitement over an advertisement for a circus. He has never seen a circus, he tells her, because his family were poor; he relates the difficulties of making his own way in life. Mrs Ramsay feels pity and compassion for him and determines to protect him from the mockery of the family; yet, at the same time, she recognizes him as 'an awful prig – oh yes, an insufferable bore'.

Mrs Ramsay makes her charitable visit to the poor. On her return Tansley is struck by her beauty, even though he realizes that she has eight children and must be at least fifty years old. He sees her 'Stepping through fields of flowers and taking to her breast buds that had broken and lambs that had fallen' (1,1,16). For a moment he sees her as a symbol of beauty, fertility, nature and creativeness. He responds with a more natural pride and feeling of joy than we have hitherto suspected he possessed.

In this first section we see Mrs Ramsay at the centre of the scene, her soothing influence on others and the way in which her children and Charles Tansley react to her; we follow her thoughts as she, in turn, reacts to her husband and Mr Tansley.

cloud what is actually at hand Spoil or impinge upon what is happening at the present moment.

any turn in the wheel of sensation i.e. any change of feeling.

Army and Navy Stores A large department store in Victoria Street, London, originally set up to supply the needs of service families.

all red and ermine on the Bench i.e. dressed in the scarlet and fur robes of a judge presiding over a court.

lean as a knife, narrow as the blade of one Similes reflecting Mr Ramsay's physique, but also suggesting his power to hurt, his keen mind, his hardness of outlook and limited vision.

the passage ... in darkness Mr Ramsay sees life as a voyage to death (that fabled land) where eventually the ships (barks) sink. The words have echoes throughout the book in the tragic events, but also in the ideas connected with the sea and the Lighthouse.

tuberculous Tuberculosis, a wasting disease, was rarely cured before the advent of antibiotics.

Hebrides A group of islands off the north-west coast of Scotland.

infidel ideas i.e. unconventional ideas.

like a queen's One of several images that suggest the regality of Mrs Ramsay's nature.

Skye A Hebridean island.

Balliol A famous college at Oxford University.

Bristol A university town in the west of England.

Bedford Bedford College, part of London University.

Prolegomena Introductory observations, usually on the subject of a book.

his acid way of peeling the flesh and blood off everything i.e. he spoke abrasively, grating on everyone's feelings, harshly dissecting their ideas.

the Reform Bill There was a series of Reform Bills passed by the British Parliaments in the nineteenth and twentieth centuries, all relating to changes in the electoral system.

The first, and most famous, was that of 1832. Others were passed in 1867, 1884 and 1918.

a valley of the Grisons A region of glaciers and peaks in the chief winter sports area of Switzerland, which includes St Moritz.

vivid streak of canary-yellow An effect believed to be caused by taking opium.

Hindustanee The language of Northern India (usually spelt 'Hundustani').

gowned and hooded i.e. wearing the gown and hood conferred by a university degree.

A fellowship A paid post of a limited tenure in a university, to undertake specific study or research.

dissertation A written paper on a special topic.

readership The office of an instructor in certain universities.

Ibsen Henrik Ibsen (1828–1906); the Norwegian playwright, author of *Hedda Gabler* and *Ghosts*.

Panama hat A summer hat, often worn in those days, which was made from a fine, almost white, straw.

the Garter The premier order of knighthood in Great Britain, membership of which is indicated by the wearing of a deep blue velvet ribbon.

Section 2

We return to the present with Tansley telling James that they will not be going to the Lighthouse. He makes an effort to soften his voice for Mrs Ramsay's benefit, but she still thinks him 'odious'.

Section 3

Mrs Ramsay reassures James about the weather and looks for a picture that he will enjoy cutting out; she finds one of a pocket knife (James had wanted to gash a hole in his father's breast when he had prophesied poor weather). She is suddenly aware of the sound of the sea and, for a moment, is terrified of the implications. Normally this sound was comforting and consoling, a symbol of permanence and stability, but now it brings to mind death and destruction. This is one of the many occasions in the book when the author demonstrates the ambiguity of life, how we respond to it with love, joy and happiness and, at other times, how it represents pain, grief, misery and pointlessness. Mrs Ramsay then hears her husband walking up and down on the terrace reciting to himself. The poetry he chooses reflects his mood of the moment; he obviously sees himself as a leader; alone, under attack, courageously battling his way through.

Lily Briscoe is the only other person to hear Mr Ramsay, and she is standing on the edge of the lawn, painting a picture of the house, showing Mrs Ramsay at the window. Mrs Ramsay does not think very highly of Lily as an artist and fears that she will never marry. She does, however, admire Lily's independent spirit.

beat a measured and soothing tattoo The waves provide a background rhythm to the whole book. Here the sea is orderly and reassuring – at other times it seems wild and chaotic.

ephemeral as a rainbow Shortlived.

a pocket knife with six blades This is used as a masculine image; Mr Ramsay was lean as a knife; James wanted to stab his father.

Stormed at with shot and shell A line from *The Charge of the Light Brigade* (1854), the famous poem by Alfred Lord Tennyson (1809–92), written to commemorate the tragic fate of the British Light Cavalry Brigade, mistakenly sent into action at the battle of Balaclava in the Crimean War, against the Russians.

Section 4

As Lily stands painting, Mr Ramsay almost strides into her as he recites to himself. She is afraid of him but is friendly to William Bankes, who comes to speak to her. They are both visitors of the Ramsays, having rooms in the village. To avoid Mr Ramsay, Mr Bankes suggests a walk; Lily agrees, but leaves her painting with reluctance.

Lily paints what she sees, and tries to keep to the truth of her vision, despite the fact that her style is unfashionable. She finds, however, that her sense of reality cannot be committed clearly to the paper. Here we have the artist's dilemma – the enormous gulf between the apprehension of what is true and significant, and its application into the form of a picture. As she paints, certain truths of her own existence are made painfully clear to Lily; she feels a sudden impulse to tell Mrs Ramsay 'I'm in love with all this.' She recognizes the absurdity of this, that 'one could not say what one meant', but we see that her painting and her feelings for Mrs Ramsay and the family, and for all Mrs Ramsay represents, are very closely connected. At the end of the book the picture is completed when Lily feels that she has some sympathetic understanding of what Mr and Mrs Ramsay were.

William Bankes and Lily look at the sea, as they do every evening: again the sea is a complex symbol. Momentarily they seem released from their individual thoughts and problems, and are filled with elation. Here again there is an alien note, a chill when they sense 'the prickly blackness' and feel 'some sadness – because the thing was completed partly'. Lily recognizes the eternity of the sea and feels her own chaotic nature and insignificance compared with 'a sky which beholds an earth entirely at rest'.

Bankes's thoughts turn to Ramsay and their friendship. After Ramsay's marriage they had gone their different ways, Ramsay becoming involved in domesticity. The friendship, however, is not dead – merely 'laid up in peat' among the sandhills. As at other moments in the book, the emphasis here is upon time, its effects, and the eternity of the significance of certain events. As Bankes continues to muse on the Ramsays, the difference between the two men is revealed: Bankes, dry and withdrawn, unattractive to children; Ramsay involved with a large family, increasingly eccentric, in need of inner moral support, with his best work behind him.

Lily regards Ramsay's work with awe. For her it is represented by a scrubbed kitchen table, the symbol of 'Subject and object and the nature of reality'. With a touch of ironic humour the author writes of Lily's 'reducing of lovely evenings, with all their flamingo clouds and blue and silver to a white deal four-legged table'. The image underlines clearly the contrast between Lily, the artist, and Mr Ramsay, the philosopher, and their very different methods of apprehending truth.

Lily responds warmly to Bankes, seeing him as pure and living for science; but then she also remembers his pettiness, and is puzzled by the contradictions in people. ('How then did it work out, all this?') Here Lily is voicing what the author feels is the central problem of personality – that it cannot be truly defined, that it is not neatly encompassed, but is chaotic, contradictory, and can only be partly understood from many impressions.

A shot from Jasper interrupts Lily's train of thought, and turning on to the terrace she and Bankes encounter Mr Ramsay, still reciting aloud, and embarrassed at being caught out in his eccentricity.

Boldly we rode and well Another line from *The Charge of the Light Brigade*.

Someone had blundered A further line from the same poem.

jacmanna Purple flowering clematis (*Clematis Jackmannii*), a climbing plant.

the Brompton Road A fashionable shopping street in the Knightsbridge district of south-west London.

red-hot pokers The common name of *Kniphophia*, a tall spiky, red or orange herbaceous border plant.

mother-of-pearl Iridescent substance that forms the inner surface of shells.

the dunes The sandhills, as opposed to the sea here, remind them of time, and therefore the end of life and their own mortality.

Westmorland A county in the Lake District of north-west England.

Like the body ... a century As he looks at the sand dunes Mr Bankes is reminded of the past and of his friendship with Mr Ramsay, which he sees preserved forever in the unchanging sands.

Sweet Alice Alyssum, a small white summer-flowering plant.

Vesuvius The large volcano overlooking Naples, in Italy.

a scrubbed kitchen table Mr Ramsay's work is symbolized by the bare, angular table, suggesting its qualities of fact and hardness; unpoetic, possibly unappealing, but solid and workmanlike.

into a pudding basin i.e. the pudding basin is placed on the head as a guideline for a basic haircut.

Section 5

Lily and Mr Bankes pass the window where Mrs Ramsay is sitting trying to measure her knitting against her son. She watches Lily and William and quite suddenly feels that they should marry. This leads to thoughts of her own marriage, the state of the house and the behaviour of her children. Again there is an emphasis on the effects of time; and the open doors of the house have a significance: there is a sense of fluidity, of change, of movement. She recalls the tragedy of the Swiss maid whose father was dying of cancer among the beautiful mountains – an event again symbolic of the nature of life; her sadness and helplessness lead to irritation with James, who will not stand still to be measured.

Though she is beautiful, there is an air of sadness about Mrs Ramsay. She is intuitive about life and people; she naturally senses and responds to all that is important – the essence, the inner core – and, in turn, she brings a sense of meaning, pleasure and fulfilment to others. But note that the author says 'falsely perhaps': there is not always pleasure, ease and fulfilment in life.

We retreat in time to Mr Bankes's feelings about Mrs Ramsay, following a telephone conversation with her from his hotel. He was aware of her beauty and stateliness, but sensed also an incongruity in harmony. Like the other characters in the book, Mr Bankes realizes that he cannot totally comprehend her character.

Mrs Ramsay's irritation with James subsides; she returns to her solicitous and loving mood, and offers to find him another picture.

heather mixture A kind of Scottish knitting wool.
criss-cross of steel needles Stockings are usually hand-knitted on four needles.
The happier Helen A reference to Helen of Troy, daughter of Zeus and wife of Menelaus, noted for her beauty. She was carried off by Paris to Troy, an act that resulted in the Trojan Wars.
Cashmere shawl A costly shawl made of fine wool, from the Kashmir, or Tibetan, goat. The green shawl of Mrs Ramsay symbolizes her soothing presence and her fruitfulness.

this swoop and fall of the spirit upon truth Emphasizes Mrs Ramsay's naturalness and intuition.

Greek Mr Bankes is still seeing Mrs Ramsay as a representative of classical beauty and love.

The Graces Three goddesses, companions to Aphrodite, whose presence spread joy and happiness. They are especially connected with the rites of spring, being associated with nature and fertility.

asphodel A kind of daffodil, said to cover the Elysian fields of classical mythology.

goloshes Rubber over-shoes (more usually spelt 'galoshes').

royalty of form A further reference to Mrs Ramsay as a goddess, or queen with a special authority and aura.

Michael Angelo (More usually 'Michelangelo': Michelagniolo Buonarroti, 1475–1564). The great Florentine sculptor, architect, painter and poet of the Renaissance; famous particularly for his statue of David in Florence and the paintings in the Sistine Chapel in the Vatican.

Section 6

Mrs Ramsay has, subconsciously, been hearing her husband's recitation, and she is aware that there is something wrong. She cannot know that he is embarrassed by having his eccentricity exposed to Bankes and Lily, and that his feeling of elation and glory has been shattered. But as he comes near she senses his anguish and respects his need for privacy and silence. She pities him and transfers her active sympathy to James instead; when she realizes her husband has calmed down, she teases him about having dismissed Charles Tansley. Here we can appreciate the sensitivity with which Mrs Ramsay is able to assess and respond to the feelings of others, and in the end create harmony.

However, the disagreement about the trip to the Lighthouse continues, with Mr Ramsay becoming enraged by his wife's illogical attitude to the weather, giving her son false hopes. His whole philosophy of life, its purpose and meaning, is called into question here, which accounts for his violent response. Mrs Ramsay's thoughts are equally violent – but she says nothing. For her, his words are destructive, brutal and insensitive, totally lacking awareness of human hopes and joy. But Mr Ramsay is obviously ashamed of his outburst and breaks the tension by offering to see the Coastguards and enquire about the weather. Immediately Mrs Ramsay, aware of his relenting, feels secure again – happy in her domesticity, looking up to him.

Mr Ramsay blunders off again, soothed by the presence of his family, and is able to ponder over a philosophical problem. Original thought is like the alphabet. In a generation, probably only one man ever reaches 'Z', ever arrives at a completely satisfactory conclusion or solution. Mr Ramsay had reached 'Q' and has been struggling to get to 'R'. He realizes he may fail. In a series of images he is compared to the saviour of a ship's company, a polar explorer and a mountaineer: the brave, tough, resourceful leader; indomitable and alone, isolated from the softness and warmth of home. But even heroes have to face failure: again the author emphasizes the ravages of time and how all lives are ultimately reduced by it. And even heroes are glad to be rescued, to have someone who will sympathize and understand their suffering. Mr Ramsay returns from the bleakness and isolation of his thoughts about 'the waste of ages and the perishing of the stars' and seeks solace in Mrs Ramsay's company – which at this moment represents 'the beauty of the world'.

Once more Virginia Woolf – having presented us with the sense of futility and pointlessness that may face us when we try to analyse and dissect the inner meaning of people and events – brings us back to the atmosphere of calm, warmth and beauty, and the knowledge that there *is* a meaning to life in the mere experiencing of it and the recognition of each experience. In this section, also, we glimpse the harmony created by Mrs Ramsay and her husband together. Each is uneasy without the support of the other, yet they are opposites in their attitudes to the world and people.

someone had blundered Again from *The Charge of the Light Brigade*; the words of the poem are linked to Mr Ramsay's own blunder of charging into Lily and William Bankes.

riding fell as a thunderbolt Mr Ramsay is enacting the events of the Charge, imagining himself as the hero in desperate conditions. The images emphasize his hardness, his masculinity and courage.

to rend the thin veils of civilization Mrs Ramsay sees her husband's insistence on telling the truth as an act of cruelty and barbarity, disregarding all the sensitivity of human feeling.

in June he gets out of tune Part of a traditional verse about the habits of the cuckoo, referring to its change of song in June prior to migrating.

the leader of a forlorn hope Throughout the passage Mr Ramsay is compared to an intrepid explorer who never gives up his expedition, however hopeless it may be.

What, indeed, if you look from a mountain-top If the leader of the expedition is successful and achieves his goal, what is that goal compared to the vastness of time? His fame and achievements will fade.

the hero puts his armour off i.e. turns away from heroic deeds and returns to ordinary life.

the waste of ages ... the stars The basis of Mrs Ramsay's
thoughts about the effects of time, and the transience of all
things.

Section 7

As his father comes to the window, demanding sympathy
from his wife, James feels hatred for him. His feelings
arise from jealousy and inadequacy compared with his
father, who is competing with him for his mother's attention and making his life more complicated.

In the following highly charged passage, Mrs Ramsay
gives her husband the support and reassurance he needs,
telling him that Charles Tansley has described him as
the greatest metaphysician of the time, thus pledging her
confidence in him. His family, friends and household are
substantial, real, and he truly is 'in the heart of life'. Mrs
Ramsay assumes here the role of the elemental female:
the figure of fertility, creativity, and the source of all
energy and life; she rises 'in a rosy-flowered fruit tree laid
with leaves and dancing boughs'.

Just as Mrs Ramsay here represents the female quality,
Mr Ramsay represents the hardness of the male. The
imagery is unmistakably sexual: 'into this delicious
fecundity, this fountain and spray of life, the fatal sterility of the male plunged itself, like a beak of brass, barren
and bare.' Mr Ramsay demands and takes and is
satisfied; Mrs Ramsay responds, gives, creates peace and
life, and is left exhausted by the process. From their
interrelationship comes 'to each that solace which two
different notes, one high, one low, struck together, seem
to give each other as they combine.' A sense of wholeness, fulfilment and joy is produced.

Yet the moment of truth passes. Mrs Ramsay feels

uneasy and exhausted. She reads James a story, and again is aware of the ominous sound of a wave falling – a reminder of time, of chaos, of bleakness. The 'pure joy' of the relationship with her husband is diminished by small burdens. She believes in him, but is aware that people disapprove of the way he leans on her; and she realizes that his last book was not his best. She knows, too, that he is eccentric. Augustus Carmichael passes the window – a reminder of the 'inadequacy of human relationships, that the most perfect was flawed'.

a rain of energy, a column of spray Images that portray Mrs Ramsay as a kind of nature goddess, a giver of life.
the fatal sterility ... barren and bare Images that reflect the harshness and violence of the male and have a sexual connotation with the above images of Mrs Ramsay.
metaphysician One versed in metaphysics, which investigates the first principles of nature and thought: the science of being.
the arid scimitar of the male Again an image that emphasizes the barren violence of men and their philosophy.
as a nurse carrying a light A comment on the relationship of Mr and Mrs Ramsay. She soothes him, gives light in a dark world.
rosy-flowered fruit tree An image of Mrs Ramsay that suggest natural fertility, life and beauty.
one petal closed in another Mrs Ramsay is here seen as a flower, folding up in exhaustion at the end of the day.
Grimm's fairy story Jacob (1785–1863) and Wilhelm (1786–1859) Grimm. German brothers, scholars and philologists who compiled a collection of German legends and folk tales. Mrs Ramsay reads one to James: 'The Fisherman's Wife', a story of the sea and a storm, and a difference of opinion between man and wife. These elements are linked with the themes of *To the Lighthouse*.

some demon in her Mrs Ramsay is upset by her husband's behaviour and reacts by speaking to Mr Carmichael – who is not overfond of her.

Section 8

Mrs Ramsay meditates on her failure with Augustus Carmichael. He has had an unfortunate marriage, and has known poverty. She believes that his wife's treatment of him is the cause of his shrinking from her. Mrs Ramsay, accustomed to everyone's admiration and affections, is hurt. Then, analysing her own feelings, she begins to suspect her motives and wonders if it is only her pride that is wounded. Again she is made aware of 'human relations, how flawed they are, how despicable, how self-seeking, at their best.' Humbled, she concentrates on reading to James, but she notices her husband pass the window.

Mr Ramsay muses on the purpose of the lives of great men. He believes that the greatest good may require the existence of a servant class. This upsets him – the average human being should be more important than one great one; the artist should not be predominant.

Mr Ramsay appears to have a conception of the need for justice in life, for equality of conditions, and to have an awareness of the importance of material things – as opposed to artistic, aesthetic creations. Yet he is not entirely sure of his conclusions. He is irritated by his failure to find a satisfactory answer. He stands 'on his little ledge facing the dark human ignorance, how we know nothing and the sea eats away the ground we stand on'. The sea here represents truth or eternity, the destructiveness of nature and of life.

Mrs Ramsay looks up and sees her husband looking

over the bay. He is like a Lighthouse, stern and solid, shining through darkness, immovable and unrelenting, yet also a symbol of security and reliability in his un-wavering truthfulness.

Mr Ramsay turns back to his wife but the comforts of domestic life are to be 'deprecated and concealed', be-cause 'he had not done the thing he might have done'. As he has not, in his work, reached the pinnacle, he is ashamed to admit pleasure in other things. It is obvious to others that he is uncertain and badly needs praise. Lily Briscoe suspects he must find it difficult to move from the world of philosophy to the world of domestic bustle.

turn to steel and adamant i.e. become hard and unfeeling.
St John's Wood A district of north-west London.
half a crown A coin worth two shillings and sixpence, today's equivalent being 12½p – which would then, of course, have bought much more than today.
acrostics Poems in which the first or last letters of each line form a word or phrase.
the Pharoahs The kings of ancient Egypt.
the tube The underground railway system of London.
the young men at Cardiff Mr Ramsay was to lecture to students at Cardiff, a university college of South Wales.
he was merely foraging and picnicking Mr Ramsay's thoughts on the terrace were relatively straightforward and familiar.
like a man who reaches from his horse Mr Ramsay sees himself as a man riding about familiar countryside, plucking roses or nuts: familiar and easy ideas. At length, however, he has to dismount and proceed on foot, alone. His thoughts become difficult; he is treading new ground.
to come out ... eating away Mr Ramsay braves the sea, the darkness, the facts of existence, the transience of life, bravely and alone.
as a stake driven ... the waves beat Mr Ramsay is

stalwart, unmoved by the sea's violence. His philosophy is
a steady rock in this world of flux.

Locke John Locke (1632–1704); English philosopher and
author of *An Essay Concerning Human Understanding*
(1690).

Hume David Hume (1711–76); Scottish philosopher and
historian, author of *Enquiry Concerning Human
Understanding* (1748).

Berkeley George Berkeley (1685–1753). Irish philosopher
and English bishop, author of *Alciphron, or the Minute
Philosopher* (1733).

come a cropper i.e. experience trouble (a metaphor taken
from horse-riding). We might say today 'come unstuck'.

Section 9

William Bankes and Lily Bricoe are still talking of Mr
Ramsay. Lily does not agree that he is a hypocrite but
she does recognize his faults. She is aware, however, of
the effect the Ramsays have on her. She is in love with
them and with what they represent: they open up the
world and make it come alive for her. They give a unity,
a meaning to her life – she lives through them.

This theme of the search for order, of the feeling of the
wholeness of life, runs through the book, as does the
opposing one of the chaotic and uncontrollable nature of
life. All the main characters have moments of complete
harmony, yet are also at times aware of darkness, ignorance, helplessness and destruction.

Love is a harmonizing factor, and Lily sees that Mr
Bankes loves Mrs Ramsay, with a pure, satisfying, un-
demanding love. She 'felt intense gratitude; for nothing
so solaced her, eased her of the perplexity of life, and
miraculously raised its burdens, as this sublime power,
this heavenly gift'. Lily herself wants to remain solitary;
but love in others helps her and her art.

Lily thinks of Mrs Ramsay, wishing she could grasp her essence, her spirit – but is it definable? She recalls Mrs Ramsay's belief that all women should marry, as 'an unmarried woman has missed the best of life'. But Lily is not like Mrs Ramsay: she is an artist, 'she liked to be herself'. Mrs Ramsay does not understand everyone, but Lily still longs to know what it is that gives her harmony and strength. She must surely have some secret, some 'tablets bearing sacred inscriptions'. Lily concludes that it is impossible to know people completely – they are 'sealed'. One can only haunt the hive like a bee, seeking and sensing, but perhaps never finally achieving complete intimacy or final knowledge.

Mr Bankes studies Lily's picture. He is interested in the technical aspect of the construction, and Lily explains that it is an abstract tribute to Mrs Ramsay and James. It celebrates something that they represent; some harmony, some inner life, some special meaning. Lily only truly comes to understand this at the end of the book, when she includes Mr Ramsay in her picture.

She has difficulty with the picture: achieving balance and unity is a problem. But as she removes the canvas from the easel she feels exhilarated: she has shared her picture with Mr Bankes. It is a moment of ecstasy, and Lily senses it is an eternal moment.

Carlyle Thomas Carlyle (1795–1881); Scottish historian and essayist, author of *The French Revolution* (1837).
like a wave ... on the beach Mr and Mrs Ramsay make Lily feel the unity of life and that she is participating in it rather than merely looking on.
white scientific coat which seemed to clothe him Lily sees Mr Bankes as a typical scientist: disinterested, unemotional and objective.
barbarity was tamed ... subdued Mr Bankes's scientific

discoveries and Mrs Ramsay's reading to James are orderly, creative and civilized.

She saw the colour ... cathedral Lily could visualize the strength and depth of meaning of her picture, see the brilliance yet delicacy of colour, sense the holiness and greatness of the subject – but she could not express it on canvas.

seek shelter under the shade Lily recognizes the strength and support of the male love for the female.

laurels Rewards.

helter skelter ... mouth Disorganized and improvident.

like a bee Lily is drawn to Mrs Ramsay as the bee to the hive.

the Kennet A river in Wiltshire.

Section 10

Cam, the young daughter, is called back by Mrs Ramsay as she runs past the window and is given a message to take to the cook, asking whether Minta Doyle and Paul Rayley have returned from their walk. Mrs Ramsay perceives that Cam is involved in her own little world and can only produce the answer – that they had not returned – with some prompting.

Mrs Ramsay returns to the story she is reading to James, and throughout this section the tale of the 'Fisherman's Wife' is interspersed with her thoughts of Minta Doyle; her own influence on people; the children; the burdens of life; her concern for James. The story itself 'was like the bass gently accompanying a tune which now and then unexpectedly ran up into the melody'. The passages quoted, which she reads to James, seem to intrude into the scene and into Mrs Ramsay's thoughts. There is the difference between husband and wife; the dominance of the woman; above all, there is the sea, powerful and stormy, partly reflecting Mrs Ramsay's unease about life and her children and partly continuing the idea of the sea's omnipresence that runs throughout the book. As Virginia Woolf noted in her diary: 'The sea is to be heard all through it.'

Mrs Ramsay hopes that the late return of the walking party means that Minta Doyle and Paul Rayley are now engaged. She has encouraged them to go out and has tried to organize the opportunity for the proposal; she feels that Minta should marry, and Paul is pleasant though not brilliant. Minta comes from a conventional, almost stultifying background, and Mrs Ramsay had invited her to Finlay in the face of the opposition of Minta's mother (who had implied that Mrs Ramsay was interfering and dominating). Mrs Ramsay defends herself from this criticism on the grounds that she would only try to impose her will where issues of social and moral importance were involved – such as the provision of hospitals and the improvement in the conditions of dairies. Even so, she reasons, with her large family she does not have the opportunity for even this kind of organizing. Is Mrs Ramsay too domineering? Certainly she tries to influence Lily, who gently resists. Generally her managing seems to result in harmony rather than stress: nevertheless, the Rayleys' marriage is not a success.

Mrs Ramsay's thoughts turn to her children, in the knowledge that they are far happier now than they can hope to be when they have to face the burdens of adulthood. Her husband accuses her of pessimism: 'with all his gloom and desperation he was happier, more hopeful on the whole, than she was.' She thinks that this is because he is less exposed to human worries. It may be, however, that through his philosophy he does in time reach a knowledge of lasting values and the enduring nature of humanity. She, on the other hand, is at the mercy of her emotions and the mundane problems of everyday family life. Her sense of life is of something to struggle with: something separate, unconquerable, always posing the eternal problems of 'suffering; death; the poor'. Life may be hostile, yet she is always driven to assert that people should marry and have children. Is this escapism, a reluctance to admit that her way of life might not be wholly the right one, that she might not be at the heart of living? Although Mrs Ramsay is vaguely conscious of her own doubts, we are able to accept, as we read on, that she is right. There is creativeness in her: by producing and encouraging new unions, new life, she is part of the force that causes humanity to endure; part of eternal truth itself.

The walkers still have not returned. Her maternal instinct aroused, Mrs Ramsay becomes afraid that Andrew may have met with an accident. But she does not allow her fears to alarm James who, as the story finishes, looks up to find that the Lighthouse lamp is lit. His wonder and imagination, stimulated by the story, are now transferred to the Lighthouse, steady and sure in the dark. His mother knows that the disappointment of not going to the Lighthouse the following day will remain with him all his life.

like the bass gently accompanying a tune The story of the sea, the storm, the difference between the man and wife, is connected with Mrs Ramsay's own present sensations.

some thorn Mrs Ramsay has an unpleasant thought: she remembers a criticism that was directed at her.

charades A game where parts of a word, or phrase, are acted, and then the whole, for the non-participants to guess.

brandishing her sword at life Mrs Ramsay feels that coming to terms with life and its problems is a battle, but one that is basically worthwhile.

Section 11

The children are in bed and Mrs Ramsay is alone. Despite her love for her family she feel that her own essential spirit can only be explored and experienced in solitude. She appreciates 'being oneself, a wedge-shaped core of darkness, something invisible to others'. There freedom lies, freedom from the humdrum pressures of domesticity, and the deeper freedom of the opportunity to settle, to exist, to rest in peace. In this inspired moment Mrs Ramsay watches the long steady third stroke of the Lighthouse and identifies herself with it. Here the Lighthouse represents steadiness, peace and immutability; it is beautiful and sternly truthful.

Suddenly she is moved to say 'We are in the hands of the Lord', and is instantly irritated at the sentimentality and superficiality of her thought, which she is aware is not true for her. She is not religious. She does not relate the evil of the world to a God.

Her husband passes the window and feels pained by her apparent remoteness. He wants to protect her – but there are things from which human beings cannot be protected. It is part of the irony in life that in wanting to help, one often hurts – as he had, in his insistence that the weather would be poor.

Mrs Ramsay sees the Lighthouse as pitiless, remorseless in its exposure of the truth – as she herself is when alone. The lovely beam of light coaxes Mrs Ramsay to respond to it. She has experienced intense happiness and exclaims: 'It is enough! It is enough.' Despite the darker side of life, one experiences enough love, delight and beauty to be fulfilled.

Mr Ramsay longs to speak to his wife now that she is alone, but he will not intrude upon her sadness. Mrs Ramsay, as always, senses his need, realizes he is too proud to come to her, so instead, she speaks to him. This scene is a splendid illustration of the real harmony of their relationship, the mute communication, the desire of both to sustain and unite.

our apparitions i.e. what we superficially appear to be.
a wedge of darkness Mrs Ramsay equates this with her inner soul, her secret true self.
a bride to meet her lover Mrs Ramsay responds to the light as a lover seeking fulfilment and union.
stroking with its silver fingers i.e. the light is personified and its tenderness wakens Mrs Ramsay to the ecstasy that is her fulfilment.

Section 12

The Ramsays stroll together through the garden, talking. They do not always agree; each has worries that cannot be shared, each is a little critical of the other, but they are sensitively aware of dangerous ground. Mr Ramsay raises her hand to his lips, kissing it 'with an intensity that brought tears to her eyes', in a gesture of love: anxious to show that he regretted nothing of their marriage, even if his books were not of the standard he might have achieved had he been alone in 'those sandhills dwindling away into darkness'. Unencumbered by a large family his philosophy might have penetrated further but he recognizes – though reluctantly – that his children compensate for his loss. They too, are his life's work and are solidly present, even though in his melancholy 'the little island seemed pathetically small, half owallowed up in the sea'. The image suggests his awareness of the insignificance of man, and the potentially evanescent nature of his work.

Mrs Ramsay is irritated by his gloomy words as she knows that in reality he is more hopeful and optimistic than she is. She dwells on his eccentricities and his blindness to the everyday happenings going on around him, yet she recognizes his fine understanding of the abstract. It must be that he is a great man, that the conventional rules do not apply to him: she is proud of him.

Lily Briscoe and William Bankes, out walking together, come into view; once again Mrs Ramsay has the thought that they should marry.

wool gathering i.e. daydreaming.

a phantom net Mrs Ramsay suddenly sees the beauty of the town and harbour lights covering all the poverty and suffering, which seems to have sunk out of sight.

those sandhills dwindling away Mr Ramsay liked the sandhills where he could be alone to face the principles of life with equanimity; the sandhills were solid and stable compared with the sea.

an eye like an eagle's Another masculine image; Mr Ramsay notices only the extraordinary, not the familiar.

Best and brightest, come away From *To Jane: The Invitation* (1822), a poem by Percy Bysshe Shelley (1792–1822).

Section 13

Mr Bankes and Lily are talking. As they turn and see the Ramsays with their children, Lily conceives them as 'symbols of marriage, husband and wife'. It is a special moment for her, almost spiritual: 'they all looked sharp-edged and ethereal and divided by great distances'. The significance lies in the harmony of the picture: parents and children together in a moment of happiness, somehow eternal. Then Mrs Ramsay, still disturbed about the walking party, asks Prue if Nancy went with them.

Rembrandt Rembrandt Harmensz van Rijn (1606–69); great Dutch painter

Prado The Spanish national museum of painting and sculpture in Madrid.

Padua The frescoes in the Avena chapel in Padua, Northern Italy, were the work of Giotto (Giotto di Bondone, 1267–1337). The frescoes depicted the lives of the Virgin Mary and Christ.

Titian Tiziano Vecelli (1477–1576); great Italian painter of the Venetian school.

Darwin Charles Darwin (1809–82); scientist and naturalist. He expounded the theory of evolution by natural selection.

for it seemed as if solidity Lily has a mystical moment when the family seem to transcend ordinary life and become symbols of unity and happiness.

Section 14

Nancy has reluctantly accompanied the others on the walk, but when Minta takes her hand she imagines she sees the world spread out before her, with pinnacles and domes: 'prominent things, without names'. She does not yet comprehend why Minta needs her as a chaperone, but she senses subconsciously that Minta is more in touch with the world, nearer the brink of life, than she is.

Andrew watches Minta's reckless abandoned behaviour. She is excited, elatedly in love, demanding attention and exaggerating her femininity in order to attract Paul Rayley. Andrew and Nancy, too young to appreciate the situation, are embarrassed and irritated.

On the beach they separate, and Nancy becomes engrossed in a rock pool: 'Brooding, she changed the pool into the sea, and made the minnows into sharks and whales'. This image suggests the changing nature and fickleness of the world: disaster may follow joy, dark will follow light, chaos will disrupt order and the vastness of the universe and time will diminish all. But notice how the sun shines in the end. Nancy is very much aware of the sea and its power, its hugeness; for a moment, she is made to see her life in relation to eternity.

As the tide comes in, Nancy and Andrew see Paul and Minta in an embrace. The children are embarrassed and awkward, even with each other; made aware of the sexual implications of the lovers' relationship. Then Minta discovers that she has lost her brooch, but her fears may also be involved in the momentous decision she has taken. The loss gives Paul Rayley the opportunity to dominate the situation, to do a great deed for his beloved. Love highlights his masculinity, makes him gallant and protective. As they return home he ponders happily on their future together, and realizes the enormousness of the decision he has taken. He had needed Mrs Ramsay to encourage him; and he is aware of the influence she exerts over him. As the house comes into view out of the darkness, his main impression is one of light. The light is his hope for the future; the brilliance of the way ahead – but it is also Mrs Ramsay and love.

Nancy, reluctantly ... beneath her Minta, about to become engaged, is part of the world now, entering into a fuller experience of life; Nancy, still a child, senses the experience awaiting her.

Constantinople The old name for Istanbul, the capital of
  Turkey.
Santa Sofia Byzantine church in Istanbul.
Golden Horn The inlet of the Bosphorus dividing
  European Istanbul.   '
Damn your eyes An old sea-shanty – again, the sea image.
she changed the pool into the sea Nancy sees the life in
  the pool as a symbol of all life, with its tragedies and
  vicissitudes.
leviathan A sea monster.
a weeping willow The willow tree is a symbol of sorrow.
  Although newly betrothed, Minta weeps; and Nancy
  knows she weeps for more than her lost brooch. Is it also
  for her change of status, her lost girlhood?

Section 15

This is a link back to the main narrative and to Mrs
Ramsay. Prue informs her that Nancy did go on the walk
with Minta and Paul.

Section 16

Mrs Ramsay dresses for dinner, still anxious about the
lateness of the return of Nancy, Andrew, Paul and Minta,
yet annoyed at the possibility of the dinner being spoiled.

  She allows Rose to select her jewellery for her. Rose
and her mother are very close; Mrs Ramsay, understanding Rose's deep feeling, is saddened by the thought of
Rose suffering when she grows up. She tries to shame
Jasper into giving up shooting rooks by pointing out their
humour, skill and sheer delight. But Jasper, the male, is
merely amused by her emotional, rather than scientific,
ideas. For him she is 'in another division of the world'.

  The walkers return at last. Mrs Ramsay descends

regally to dinner, aware of herself as their spiritual centre, supremely conscious of her own beauty – the outward symbol of the inner influence.

The day has brought many things. Individual thoughts have taken on lives of their own. People have attempted to influence others; some have argued; some have just followed their own interests. Now they are to be brought together by Mrs Ramsay's dinner.

Boeuf en Daube An old French dish: beef cooked in wine, with herbs.

Joseph and Mary For Mrs Ramsay the rooks have an almost religious significance – they promise stability.

Section 17

The dinner party is the climax of Part 1. Fourteen people in varying moods come to the table, some reluctantly, some late. Each one only thinly disguises his irritation or aloofness, and the atmosphere at first is cold and fragmented. Mrs Ramsay is tired and feels 'past everything, through everything, out of everything'. She knows that nothing seems to have come together, but she is too passive to do anything about it just yet.

Charles Tansley is irritable, believing himself to be above this kind of 'damned rot', desiring only to find some conversation wherein he could show off his intellectual powers. Mr Bankes thinks the occasion a 'terrible waste of time'. He has agreed to attend for Mrs Ramsay's sake but he would much prefer to be concentrating on his scientific work. Lily is ruffled by Tansley's superior attitude to women and she teases him. Mr Ramsay grows openly angry and scowls when Mr Carmichael, oblivious of everyone else, begins the soup course again.

Everyone's thoughts are revealed, many of them

covering a wide range of emotions before the end of the meal, particularly those of Mrs Ramsay. Each member of the dinner party has his or her own complexity, adopting not just one attitude but several, some of them contradictory. The author's technique of presenting character realistically is seen at its best here. The personalities interrelate, are influenced by others and react to others. The men's behaviour is essentially different from that of the women. At first Mrs Ramsay is aware of the 'sterility' of the men, of their hardness; and she forces herself to work on them, to soften them, to make them harmonize. Both Lily and Minta eventually contribute to easing the atmosphere: Lily is kind to Tansley and Minta flirts with Mr Ramsay.

Mrs Ramsay feels sorry for the old widower William Bankes, and she brings him into the conversation; but Lily, seeing more clearly, realizes Mrs Ramsay is mistaken: Bankes is in no need of pity, fulfilled as he is by his work. At the thought of work Lily suddenly understands how she might improve her picture. Throughout the meal, in moments of stress, she returns to the idea of her painting. It is symbolic – almost as though she is outside the main stream of action and feeling – but, as a creative artist, she is able to represent that life for posterity. She teases Charles Tansley, noting his egotism, his desire to assert himself; when he senses her insincerity, he feels humiliated. Tansley believes they are laughing at him, and Lily recognizes that it is her social responsibility to soothe his discomfiture; she is forced, in the end, to play out the role, by Mrs Ramsay who mutely seeks her help in easing the atmosphere. Lily speaks kindly to Tansley, but knows that she does so without sincerity – as an artist she seeks the truth above all.

We see throughout the book that each character can

only be completely true, honest and frank when alone. Society and relationships would become dislocated by the total truth, yet each person seeks and finds truth of a kind.

Meanwhile Mrs Ramsay has been talking to Mr Bankes about the Mannings, who are old friends. It disturbs her to know that so much has happened that is not due to her influence. She senses that the scenes of the past are secure and ordered, and 'lay, like a lake, placidly between its banks'. It is the unknown future that is frightening, rather than the past, which is patterned and familiar.

Mr Bankes, for the moment, is untouched by Mrs Ramsay's influence and is not kindly disposed towards her. She has, by causing him to come to dinner, provided him with time to think, and his thoughts are uncomfortable. 'Is human life this? Is human life that?' This is, of course, the question at the heart of the book, and is one with which Virginia Woolf is concerned in all her novels.

The conversation turns to the fishermen. Charles Tansley speaks forcibly: his grandfather was a fisherman and he knows his subject. Mr Bankes is drawn into the discussion, recognizing the young man's vigour and promise. Mrs Ramsay wishes her husband would make some contribution, he would be so fervent, the topic would come alive. But he is preoccupied by his annoyance with Augustus Carmichael, who sits so placidly, seemingly unimpressed by any of them.

Mrs Ramsay has managed to relieve the tension a little. Tansley is now enjoying himself; she has involved Mr Bankes in the talk: there remains the imminent laughter of the children, the aloofness of Mr Carmichael and the rage of Mr Ramsay to be dealt with. She orders the candles to be lit and suddenly the light cuts out the dark and there is a feeling of community, a pattern round the table. The climax of the dinner is approaching. Mrs Ramsay and Augustus Carmichael have a moment of communion in their pleasure at the arrangement of the bowl of fruit: a symbol of fertility, of life. At last they are united.

Significantly, the main dish, the classic Boeuf en Daube, and the newly betrothed pair arrive together. Minta represents the triumphant female and her magic power: 'She wore her golden haze.' She is elated by love and feels expansive towards all men. She flirts with Mr Ramsay and arouses his protective feelings by making 'herself out even more ignorant than she was'. In responding to her he seems a young man again, 'not burdened, not weighed down with the greatness of his labours and the sorrows of the world'. Love is a powerful force here, softening all around it.

Mrs Ramsay finds Paul, the non-intellectual, charming. His joy is clear and she realizes that the engagement is a fact. She turns to serve the Boeuf en Daube, feeling she is 'celebrating a festival' – the festival of love – but she also sees the two 'entering into illusion glittering eyed'. 'It is a triumph,' Mr Bankes says, referring to the dish, but for Mrs Ramsay the engagement is also a triumph. It is almost a religious moment for her; to keep alive the illusion, to underline the sanctity of love and the future of life itself.

The Boeuf en Daube symbolizes the life-giving warmth of the family party. Mrs Bankes not only agreed to attend, but is now actually enjoying himself, and the tenderness of the meat rekindles his *tendresse* towards Mrs Ramsay.

Lily is both fascinated and awed by Mrs Ramsay's power, and frightened by this strange force at the centre of life: the force that Mrs Ramsay worships and represents. She even sees the engaged couple as Mrs Ramsay's 'victims', led to the altar. The question is posed: is this a celebration or a sacrifice? It is both. As she talks to Paul she realizes he is ruthless in his love and, unable to feel that kind of love herself, sensing it as 'degradation' or 'dilution' she reverts to thinking of her picture again. Here the author explores the nature of love, which is 'so beautiful, so exciting' but which is also the 'stupidest, the most barbaric of human passions'. Like life itself, it is ambiguous, incongruous and contradictory; yet it is a shaping force.

The dinner party continues well. Mrs Ramsay is at the centre of the happiness she has created. She is aware, however, that neither Lily nor Tansley can join in this celebration of love, but hopes that Tansley's dissertation will suffice for him. She considers how Lily and William Bankes may, like Paul and Minta, be brought together.

Then Mrs Ramsay senses discord. The men are arguing about Scott's novels. Mr Ramsay is made uneasy by the question 'how long do you think it'll last?' It reminds him of his own position, his own work. The situation is relieved when Minta instinctively changes the subject; Mrs Ramsay is then upset by Rose removing a pear from the bowl of fruit, spoiling its symmetry. She ponders on the differences in her children, the separateness of their lives apart; yet realizing how moved Prue is by the love of Minta and Paul. Mrs Ramsay is happy again: everything is harmonious after all. Even Augustus Carmichael is reciting poetry with Mr Ramsay. 'Without knowing why, she felt that he liked her better than he had ever done before.' At the end of the dinner she leaves the room, with a feeling of gratitude.

This scene has demonstrated the manner in which Mrs Ramsay has achieved order out of chaos, concord out of discord. Each person at the table has, in the end, responded to another with some enthusiasm and warmth. People are shown as complex and changing. Mrs Ramsay herself experiences pessimism and boredom; pity and uncertainty; pleasure and irritation; anxiety, interest, nostalgia, and dislike. The poem at the end is significant. Life is flux, life is complex; things change – but it is also stimulating and beautiful.

eddy A small current flowing in a different direction from the main current: Mrs Ramsay suddenly feels out of things.

the little shake that one gives a watch Mrs Ramsay had seemed out of life, out of time. She forces herself to start functioning again.

as a sailor ... sees the wind fill his sail Mrs Ramsay takes up her main functions of life again. The sea image of life or time is recurrent.

a fading ship Lily also sees Mrs Ramsay as voyaging, though to places where she cannot follow. Lily is detached, observing rather than participating.

dress clothes Clothes worn for formal dinners etc.

Marlow A small Buckinghamshire town on the River Thames.

gliding like a ghost Mrs Ramsay remembers people from the past. For her the past is the reality, their present selves are meaningless as she has not seen them for many years.

He felt rigid and barren, like a pair of boots Mr Bankes feels nothing for Mrs Ramsay. He seems dried up and unreceptive.

bear garden A place full of confusion.

dished himself i.e. spoilt his own chances.

the ribs and thigh bones of the young man's desire i.e. the outline or basic elements of his feeling.

Mr Tansley raised a hammer He longs to attack Lily, to crush her verbally.

he could not smite that butterfly i.e. he could not bring himself to speak savagely to a creature of so little importance!

apply some balm Soothe.

life will run upon the rocks i.e. life will be hazardous and difficult.

life . . . lay, like a lake, placidly between its banks The life of the plast is known and unchangeable, and therefore safe, unlike the 'cascades' of the present which will lead one into the unknown.

a trophy fetched from the bottom of the sea Mrs Ramsay sees the dish of fruit as a symbol of the pleasures of life, of the fertility of life and its profundity of experience.

Neptune God of the sea in classical mythology, the inheritor of the kingdom of Poseidon.

Bacchus Classical god of wine and feasting.

outside, a reflection, in which things wavered and vanished. An island of warmth and stability has been created inside the room; outside, like the sea, all is restless.

George Eliot (1819–80): great English novelist, whose real name was Mary Ann Evans; her greatest work was *Middlemarch* (1871–2).

entering into illusion glittering eyed Although Mrs Ramsay celebrates the love of Paul and Minta, still she knows with certainty that it will fade, that their ecstasy will not endure.

led her victims, Lily felt, to the altar Lily feels that despite Mrs Ramsay's worship of love and marriage, she knows very well that Paul and Minta's union could be a sort of sacrifice to life.

exposed to those fangs Lily sees Paul's love as ferocious and consuming.

a bully with a crowbar Paul is emboldened by his love, exhibiting a vicious streak to anyone he considers irrelevant.

vail her crest i.e. submit.

she hovered . . . an element of joy Mrs Ramsay is elated and supported by the natural feeling of communion and union that she senses all about her.

Voltaire Jean François Marie Arouet de Voltaire (1694–1778); French satirist, philosopher, historian, dramatist and poet.

Madame de Staël Anne Louise Germaine Necker, Baronne de Staël-Holstein (1766–1817); French novelist and essayist, celebrated for her 'salons' attended by leading literary and political figures of the day.

Lord Rosebery (1847–1929); Foreign Secretary in two of Gladstone's governments.

Creevey's Memoirs Thomas Creevey (1768–1838); a Whig Member of Parliament whose *Creevey Papers*, when published, threw light on various prominent personalities of the time.

Waverley novels A series of thirty-two novels and tales by Sir Walter Scott. The first, *Waverley*, gave its name to the others, and is a historical novel set in Scotland.

Sir Walter Sir Walter Scott (1771–1832); a famous Scottish writer of historical and romantic novels, some of which are fine records of Scottish life.

Jane Austen (1775–1815); one of the great English novelists, author of *Pride and Prejudice* and *Emma*.

Tolstoi Count Leo Tolstoi (1828–1910); Russian novelist and philosopher, author of *War and Peace* and *Anna Karenina*.

Vronsky The soldier in *Anna Karenina* for whom Anna abandons her husband and son.

voices at a service in a cathedral To Mrs Ramsay the family gathering seems like a celebration of something holy and reverent: life itself.

Luriana Lurilee The words are from the poem *Luriana Lurilee* by Charles Elton (1839–1900), who was related by marriage to Lytton Strachey, a close friend of Virginia Woolf.

he did her homage He acknowledged and respected her powers, aware of what she had achieved.

Section 18

After dinner Mrs Ramsay goes upstairs. Lily notices that when she departs 'a sort of disintegration set in'. Mrs

Ramsay needs to be alone, to consider the significance of the engagement. She notices with relief the steadiness of the club, for the 'events had given her a sense of movement.' She sees the betrothal as a symbol of rebirth; in Paul and Minta's new lives together, she and her house and her family would, in a sense, live on, forever a significant part of them. Here is her motive for encouraging those around her to marry; it is an instinct for the survival of all that is good, that lies at the heart of mankind.

Mrs Ramsay tends her children and reveals her natural maternal instincts. Cam is frightened by the sheep's skull; James wants to keep his treasure. The girl is emotional; the boy more scientific. Their mother achieves a compromise. She talks to Cam of the magical gifts of nature, underlining her own symbolic power.

She returns downstairs, and Prue feels it is good for Paul and Minta to see her mother – the symbol of motherhood and of married happiness. Mrs Ramsay encourages them all to go down to the beach, taking pleasure in Paul's success and in her thoughts humorously concentrating on his gold watch in a wash-leather bag. She does not accompany them: instinct holds her back. They must now go forward on their own to look at the sea, to experience life.

it was all one stream Mrs Ramsay, in a happy emotional state, feels communion with all mankind. She senses the unity of life; past, present and future.

Section 19

Mrs Ramsay returns to her husband, who is engrossed in a Scott novel. He is reading to determine whether the writer is still valid in the present, concerned as he is about his own status. The lines of *Luriana Lurilee* float through Mrs Ramsay's mind; she picks up a book of poetry and reads at random.

In this passage (where Mr and Mrs Ramsay are reading), Virginia Woolf explores the nature of literature, of art. Mr Ramsay is much moved, elated and fortified, lifted out of his own troubles by the simplicity and strength of the novel. Mrs Ramsay is stirred by the images in the poems she is reading: they reflect her own experiences. She recognizes 'the essence sucked out of life and held rounded here – the sonnet'. For both of them, art expresses life, not in all its chaotic muddle but formulated, and with meaning. This is what the author attempts in all her novels and what Lily Briscoe does in her painting.

Mr Ramsey enjoys the sense of quiet sympathy between his wife and himself. They discuss the engagement, but Mrs Ramsay wonders, 'Why is it then that one wants people to marry?' She needs reassurance and is given it by his dislike of her pessimism. He must be right. She believes the marriage will succeed. Here we see clearly that it is her *instinct* that guides her towards marriage for everyone: her intellect would doubt its certain value.

Mrs Ramsay becomes conscious that her husband too is in need of reassurance. Moved by her beauty, and the events of the day, he needs her love. She cannot tell him in words, but she smiles and acknowledges that he is right about everything – which is enough. Their mutual love brings back her joy and removes her doubts: 'Nothing on earth can equal this happiness.' At the end of the day their love has triumphed again. In the previous chapter the power of love affected the characters in different ways; here, it binds two very contrasting individuals together, supplying each with greater strength and joy.

the fine gravings i.e. the lines of Mrs Ramsay's face, which resembled engravings.

sinking deeper Mrs Ramsay feels her consciousness sinking into water, as it were. She is deeply involved; feels she is at the heart of life.

Steer, hither steer your winged pines From *The Siren's Song* by William Browne (1591–1643).

Mucklebackit, Steenie Characters from *The Antiquary* (1816), a novel by Sir Walter Scott.

Balzac Honoré de Balzac (1799–1850). Great French novelist.

Nor praise the deep vermilion ... As with your shadow From a sonnet by William Shakespeare (1564–1616), which begins: 'From you have I been absent in the spring' (No 98).

crepuscular Dim, as at dusk.

Revision questions on Part 1

1 Look at the structure of the first part. Show what devices are used to link separate characters and incidents together.

2 What do we learn of the relationship between James and (a) his mother, (b) his father, in the first part?

3 Study the figurative language describing Mr Ramsay in Part 1. What impressions do we gain of him?

4 Compare Mr Ramsay and Charles Tansley.

5 Describe how Mrs Ramsay's influence produces a successful dinner-party.

6 Outline Mrs Ramsay's thoughts on time and its effect on human life.

7 Show how the author incorporates past scenes and events into the narrative; discuss the purpose and significance of these.

8 Discuss the significance of the part title 'The Window'.

9 Show how any *two* characters from Part 1 display inconsistency.

10 What moments of significant human friendship and relationship are described in Part 1, and what makes them important?

11 How does the outer Mrs Ramsay differ from the inner one, that 'wedge-shaped core of darkness'?

12 Discuss the significance of the scene on the beach in relation to the first part of the book.

13 Show how Lily is, bascially, drawn as a contrast to Mrs Ramsay.

14 What is Lily's function in the first part of the book?

15 Indicate how the quotations from literature are closely linked to moods, feelings and situations and add to their significance.

Part 2   Time Passes

Section 1

The family and visitors return indoors from the terrace and the beach; and what is said now provides poetic links with the themes and events of the rest of this section of the novel

It is dark; they cannot see, the lamps are extinguished. 'One can hardly tell which is the sea and which is the land.' The forces of night and chaos move in.

Virgil Roman poet (70–19 BC) and author of the *Aeneid*.

Section 2

Everyone is in bed. The rain falls; darkness falls, too, like a flood. It is alive, personified. It permeates the house and rules, obliterating all individuality, all material things, turning everything to 'nothingness'. 'Certain airs' slip into everything; one might imagine them questioning. When will the wallpaper fall? When will the roses on it fade? How long will the letters, flowers, books, endure? The night and the airs represent time. We cannot see the future but there will be death: of people and of ideas; there will be decay of everything once so beautiful, precious and important.

But as the airs come upon them in their beds, there is a note of optimism: individuals may die but the human race will endure. What these people stand for will live.

Nothing stirred Almost a personification of 'certain airs', emphasizing the emptiness and hollowness of the night.

Section 3

In a highly poetic style Virginia Woolf describes how one night turns to many, and time passes. She is saying how insignificant one night, or one life, is – when set against all the nights and lives of time. Yet in the darkness of time there appears to be light; that is, hope, goodness, joy. Note the 'plates of brightness' in the winter; the 'flash of tattered flags'; the 'gold letters on marble pages'. Amongst chaos we see images of life, fulfilment and delight. Yet these are not to be ours for ever. 'Divine Goodness' stipulates otherwise, and the brightness is drenched, confused and fragmented.

The whole of this passage sees life – particularly its sorrowful side – through a poet's eyes. We seek some meaning and order to life, knowledge that it is all for a purpose and not totally random. The 'Divine Goodness' acts here as a force of fate connected with time. Fate turns joy to grief, life to death, and hope to despair.

So time passes and is destructive. There is nothing in the next few years that brings 'the night to order'. In the confusion, what is the point of asking 'what, and why, and wherefore'? Events seem to be pointless. Mr Ramsay must feel this when Mrs Ramsay dies suddenly. His arms stretch out, empty, and there seems no reason.

Note the way in which this important part of the narrative is written tersely and in parenthesis, emphasizing that the death of one person is of only minimal importance in the halls of time. It also underlines the author's inclination towards people's thoughts and personalities, rather than the story and action, as the interesting aspect of the book. The traditional novel would treat Mrs Ramsay's death as the climax, developed in detail, but here it is the thoughts of those who remain that count.

holds a pack of them The nights are seen as a pack of cards dealt out by winter. This emphasizes the fact that fate governs life; man seems powerless.

Section 4

The house in Scotland lies empty and has suffered the effects of time. Now, however, it is seen in the light (though there are shadows too) where 'loveliness reigned and stillness, and together made the shape of loveliness itself, a form from which life had parted'. Mrs Ramsay is dead but her influence and meaning live on. The house remains, and in its silence are woven sounds of everyday life. It is stable, awaiting the future. The shadow wavers and Mrs McNab, the slightly demonic charlady, throws open all the windows and lets in light and air.

After the chapter concerned with confusion and despair, comes the passage of hope, peace, an assurance that life *is* ordered, that after night comes day.

advance guards of great armies The house seems to be besieged and attacked by the forces of nature.

Loveliness and stillness clasped hands in the bedroom Beauty is personified and lives on despite the surrounding decay. We are reminded of Mrs Ramsay, who, though dead, lives on as an influence.

Section 5

Mrs McNab represents a kind of comic life-pattern. She lurches through the house as the airs had slid; she restores where the airs had decayed. In her grotesqueness there is an unyielding force – witless though it may be – as she clutches, rolls, leers, hobbles and creaks. She lives and enjoys by sheer instinct. She has suffered; she is old and weary, battered by life; yet she smiles and sings 'as if, indeed, there twined about her dirge some incorrigible hope'. She has none of the insight of the mystic but she drinks and gossips and experiences pleasures fully. This chapter illustrates the author's humour. With a beautiful irony she sees mankind's persistence in living and hoping, and its resilience. Nevertheless, in her irony there is also pathos and sympathy. Mrs McNab is part of the splendour of humanity.

base-born Of lowly birth, or illegitimate; here the meaning is illegitimate.

Section 6

This section covers three years, during which tragedy strikes the Ramsay family, the sadness being reflected in the descriptions of nature and the seasons. First comes spring – bare and infertile it seems – and we learn that Prue Ramsay is married. With summer the fullness of the season suggests 'that good triumphs, happiness prevails, order rules', yet somehow there is unease, a warning note that all is not as secure as it seems. The following spring 'veiled her eyes, averted her head' because of 'a knowledge of the sorrows of mankind'. Summer comes, and with it the knowledge that Prue Ramsay has died in childbirth.

The following spring the Lighthouse shines softly again, a symbol of peace; but in summer there are ominous sounds, the noise of falling, and we learn that Andrew Ramsay has been killed in the war (World War I, 1914–18).

Once again the author demands: how can we reconcile the beauty and the ugliness of life? The serenity of nature is touched by 'the ashen-coloured ship', or 'the purplish stain'. Joy is marred by sorrow; the dream of seeking perfect happiness is shattered.

The chapter ends with the news – in parenthesis – of Mr Carmichael's successful volume of poems. It is a small event, but at least a totally happy one.

of flesh turned to atoms which drove before the wind A mystical dissolution of the body into an ecstatic sensation of pure energy.

of stars flashing in their hearts The light of happiness, beauty or fulfilment in their minds.

the spring ... veiled her eyes, averted her head A personification of spring who has knowledge of the tragedy to come.

measured blows of hammers The sounds in the house causing disintegration are linked with the sounds of World War I, where Andrew Ramsay is killed in France.

there was a purplish stain ... the sea Nature seems to reflect the violence of man's actions.

Section 7

This passage describes the horror of the storms 'pierced by no light of reason', and the strangeness of the spring that followed; blooming 'yet beholding nothing, eyeless and so terrible'. Happiness has not yet entirely returned but the way for it is being prepared.

Section 8

In the house in Scotland Mrs McNab is trying to halt the rot, to keep the place in order, but is finding it too much. She feels the family should come to see for themselves what is happening, but she is aware of the difficulties of the war years. She has a clear memory of Mrs Ramsay, with her flowers and her children; she still seems to be present 'like a yellow beam or the circle at the end of a telescope'. There have been great changes, both in the house and in the family. The years have passed but Mrs Ramsay's memory remains; and the house now needs the family to return – or it will decay irrevocably.

Michaelmas The Feast of St Michael, traditionally the 29 September.
like a yellow beam The picture of Mrs Ramsay is distanced by time; she appears smaller, but note the shining quality of her memory.

Section 9

The house is on the brink of reverting to nature. Toads, swallows, rats, butterflies, poppies and weeds have taken over. 'What power could now prevent the fertility, the insensibility of nature?' The issue is in the balance. The Lighthouse shines impersonally over the scene. If no one comes the house will fall.

But 'there was a force working; something not highly conscious'. The two charwomen prepare the house once more for a visit, but something more is implied. Fate decrees that all will not revert to chaos, that order will prevail. There is also a spirit at work in the family: the force of endurance, persistence and renewal of hope. Life goes on; the house will be occupied once more.

As the charwomen work they stay 'the corruption and rot', and there is a sense of 'some rusty laborious birth'. There is 'conquest' and 'triumph'. At one level this is the restoration of the house to cleanliness and order, yet it also represents a triumph over despair and disintegration: the human achievement of producing form and wholesomeness out of disorder and confusion. Mrs McNab remembers Mr Ramsay, seeing him in a 'ring of light'. He will be at the centre of the next part of the book, as Mrs Ramsay was at the centre of the first part.

As the house is restored, the silence goes; one is half aware of the sounds of life, 'that intermittent music', and a sense of harmony is suggested. With the darkness of night there is no longer confusion and nothingness, but peace and a sense of life conveyed by the green leaves and white flowers.

Finally, Lily Briscoe and Augustus Carmichael return to the house. The wheel has turned full circle.

some rusty laborious birth The house is reborn to life. The pieces of the past are to be picked up. The younger generation will go on, and will make the trip to the Lighthouse.

She watched her son George scything A scythe is sometimes used as a symbol for the passing of time.

Section 10

The war is over. Peace has come, and as Lily lies down to sleep she is most aware of the tranquillity of the house, the night, and the voice of the sea murmuring its beauty to the world. Mr Carmichael believes things are much as they always were (despite the tragedies of the previous ten years). So 'why not accept this, be content with this, acquiesce and resign?' The miseries of life are dimmed when they are over; solace and even joy can be found in what remains.

The next morning Lily sits up. 'Awake'. She is the artist; she is alive and awake to the realities and the potential of life.

night flowing down in purple Lily sees night now as beautiful and majestic, different from the previous stormy destructive nights.

the sun ... broke the veil on their eyes Night lifts, gloom lifts, the sun brings a new day and a new awareness.

Revision questions on Part 2

1 Write a description of the atmosphere that Virginia Woolf creates in any sequence or sequences in this part.

2 What do you find poetic in this part? Quote in support of your answer.

3 Show how Virginia Woolf marks the passage of time by indicating the main events which have occurred.

4 What do you find sad about this part of the novel?

Part 3 The Lighthouse

Section 1

'What does it mean then, what can it all mean?' This reflects Lily's puzzling about the significance of the past, of the personalities of the Ramsays, and indeed about life in general. The book works towards an answer of some kind – though not a complete one – through Lily's consciousness and her painting.

She is disturbed by the general upheaval in the house. Mr Ramsay is to take Cam and James to the Lighthouse, and they are unwilling and unready. In his 'What's the use of going now?' Mr Ramsay unconsciously reflects Lily's 'What does one do?' Lily thinks it is 'as if the link that usually bound things together had been cut'. It is Mrs Ramsay that is missing: to organize, do what is needed and restore unity to the family. Lily is deadened. She remembers the three deaths and feels nothing: as yet the past has no meaning.

Mr Ramsay strides angrily about, reciting verse. 'Alone,' she hears him say; 'Perished,' she hears him say. The words are symbolic of his position without Mrs Ramsay. Lily, aware of the fragmentation of the family, remembers her picture. She will paint it again. It is through her art that a sense of unity will eventually be created for her.

It is not only through Lily's picture that fulfilment is achieved but also through the journey to the Lighthouse, a journey that is both real and symbolic. At this point Lily is horrified by the tyranny of Mr Ramsay, imposing his will on Cam and James, who are forced to go with him. She finds it difficult to paint when he is near; she is enraged at his masculine force. She accepts that she will have to give, as Mrs Ramsay has given. But Lily is not the full-blossoming female that Mrs Ramsay was; she does not respond to the male as Mrs Ramsay did. Lily wished to remain aloof, unscorched, but she realizes that something will be demanded of her. Perhaps she can imitate the 'self-surrender' of other women; but the reward will give her no pleasure. To be able to resume her painting she is forced to confront Mr Ramsay and it is only after this happens, and the final welling up of sympathy and appreciation that she feels for him, that Lily can complete her picture. It is as if the artist has to come to terms with the male spirit, as well as the female, to achieve an all-embracing view of life.

Section 2

Mr Ramsay bears down on Lily, demanding sympathy. Bereft of Mrs Ramsay, he needs a woman's appreciation. When Lily remains silent he groans aloud, dramatizing his sorrow. Lily is revolted by his egotism. The author's sense of humour is shown here in her description of Lily's primness and Mr Ramsay's absurdly exaggerated behaviour. At last Lily responds, not to his suffering but, comically, to his boots! As an artist she approves of their 'sculptured' look. Amazingly, Mr Ramsay is delighted – he too is very proud of his boots! His attention distracted, he becomes softer and more compliant, and Lily suddenly grasps the pathos of his situation. At last she is able to see him in proportion. She is willing to give now, but realizes that Mr Ramsay has to go on alone. The spiritual nature of that journey to the Lighthouse is suggested here. Without his wife, he must face life, must conquer his own despair and his desire to lean on others.

Cam and James join their father reluctantly. Lily, now seeing Mr Ramsay as a leader, watches them go; they make a stern group, with the children suffering and the father determined and courageous. Mr Ramsay is a reflection of his work. Lily recognizes now his asceticism, his pursuit of truth, his visionary quality. At the same time she understands his doubts about himself and his work. Because of the boots she has discovered his simplicity and humanity; but she also recognizes the greatness in him, his spiritual nature.

Alone ... Perished From the poem *The Castaway*, written shortly before his death by William Cowper (1731–1800). Mr Ramsay feels deserted and tragically alone after the death of his wife.

Section 3

In the previous Section we have seen Lily contemplating Mr Ramsay's character. Now it is his turn to appraise Lily: 'She seemed to have shrivelled slightly ... a little skimpy, wispy; but not unattractive.'

He regrets having been out of temper with her at breakfast; now he urgently needs her sympathy. He approaches her with solicitous questions as to her comfort and well-being at the house. Lily, though aware of his need for sympathy, is made nervous and cannot respond as she would like to. She is alarmed by the desperation she sees in his face, and by 'the immense pressure of his concentrated woe' – and ashamed of her own inability to meet his needs with words of praise and sympathy.

Cam and James arrive on the terrace, reluctantly prepared to accompany their father to the Lighthouse. Lily feels angry with them for their grudging attitude towards their father; and at last feels sympathy for him. But the gate bangs, and he has gone with his children on the journey to the Lighthouse.

heavy draperies of grief Lily sees Mr Ramsay as if he were in the black clothes of mourning, flaunting his grief.
crape The black material used for mourning clothes, or for a band round a mourner's hat.
all she did ... round her ankles An image suggesting

Lily's primness, and her fear of participation in the emotional turmoil of life.

pall Black or purple cloth draped over a coffin.

They had reached . . . where peace dwelt Lily sees the relationship between herself and Mr Ramsay as a voyage which has ended happily, just as the voyage to the Lighthouse will.

There was no helping Mr Ramsay Lily could do nothing for Mr Ramsay either on his visit to the Lighthouse or on his journey through life; everyone must finally stand alone.

a leader ... expedition Once again Mr Ramsay is seen heroically. The journey to the Lighthouse is a great undertaking; it has deep significance.

He must have had his doubts The kitchen table (as a symbol of Mr Ramsay's work, of philosophic truth) is mentioned again. He had moments when its value and reality were doubtful.

he was like a lion A further image suggesting fierceness and strength.

Section 4

Lily begins to paint but finds it difficult, beset by the problems involved with any work of art: the gap between idea and execution, between subject and object. Soon, however, a rhythm is created, things become more related, a pattern emerges (we are reminded of the symbol of the Lighthouse in its light, dark rhythm). Lily feels that she is separated from real life, above it. She is the artist, seeing life in proportion, summing it up at a distance.

As she paints, she begins to understand the inner meaning of people and events. Although Charles Tansley had irritated her, the incident of their flash of friendship and rapport on the beach stands clearly in her memory, and she feels that this moment has endured. She attributes this to Mrs Ramsay who, she feels, created the harmonious conditions in the first place.

Lily continues painting and thinking of Mrs Ramsay. But she has to find out what is happening to the Lighthouse party: the progress of her picture is now linked to the progress of the boat. Like Lily, the boat was set apart. Just as Lily had experienced difficulties with her picture, so the boat moves hesitantly at first but eventually it sails on firmly out to sea.

tied a knot in her mind i.e. stayed clearly in her memory.

she attained a ... movement Lily becomes immersed in the sea of sensation and feeling.

she had a few moments ... unborn soul Lily's painting will expose her inner self and will give birth to the expression of her soul.

this rhythm was strong The rhythm of the Lighthouse, of night and day, of the seasons and of the sea – of life itself, flows through the whole book. Lily expresses this in her painting.

ducks and drakes A game where one throws flat stones onto water, making them bounce.

like a work of art Mrs Ramsay had created the moment of friendship between Charles and Lily, whole, satisfying and full of meaning.

illuminations, matches, struck unexpectedly Life is not a great revelation but there are unexpected moments of insight.

Section 5

Cam and James are angry. They are unfriendly to their father and determined to oppose him. They can foresee that they will be embarrassed by their father's excitement and lack of inhibitions with the fishermen. Macalister, the boatman, recalls the great storm at Christmas, how three men had drowned and three ships had sunk. There are echoes of the three deaths in the Ramsay family. Mr Ramsay relishes the story; the idea of masculine daring and the bravery of the men facing the vicissitudes of life appeals to him.

But as Cam watches him she is stirred by some of his qualities, though she remembers 'those rites he went through'. He is tied to the dead: she is young and hates the bonds of the past. As she looks at the island it seems far away. This is symbolic of her past: it is the present that is reality, going on is all that matters. She has already enquired where they are going. They are going to the Lighthouse; but they are also going on to make good lives for themselves – released from the tyranny of past feelings, events and people.

Mr Ramsay dwells on the past, once again dramatizing his tragedy, reciting sorrowful poetry aloud. Just as Cam has softened a little towards him, so he wants to make contact with her. He is irritated, then amused, by the vagueness of her mind – she has no idea of the points of the compass. She is, he thinks, typically feminine, and he wants her to smile. Suddenly he decides to become less demanding, more giving, and tries to please her.

Cam is perplexed. The alternatives in life are not easy. She must resist the tyrant, yet 'no-one attracted her more' than her father. She admires him and is drawn to him but the unreasonable demands made upon her as a child and his domineering nature are still repulsive to her. She would respond to his friendliness but is aware of James's sternness. There is James's justice on the one hand and her love for her father on the other. One response seems negative – the silence, the rebuffing, the unyielding; the other – the answering, and love – is the more positive. James may have appeared god-like but Mr Ramsay is human and cries out for human responses. One is to the intellect, the other to the emotions. James is the male, the intellectual; Cam is female, tending towards the emotional. One is barren, the other fertile.

But I beneath a rougher sea Again from *The Castaway*.
James the lawgiver His mother had visualized him as a
  judge. Cam sees him as representing justice.

Section 6

Lily watches the boat, conscious of the dichotomy between parent and children. Mr Ramsay is alone, and she cannot reach him. She has not shown him the sympathy he has aroused in her. She knows she is different from people like Minta, and she feels the need to talk to Mr Carmichael, who is basking on the lawn. He is a poet, as she is an artist – the same kind of people.

The incident on the beach from former years comes to Lily's mind again and she remembers Mrs Ramsay's silence. As she paints Lily ponders over the meaning of the past – the significance of particular moments, how to grasp and define them and create a whole from their scattered parts. She thinks of relationships and life in general. Her thoughts are linked to the progress of her picture; as life's experiences begin to reveal their meaning, so will the picture improve. In her search for truth and purpose Lily has an affinity with Mr Ramsay, even with the Lighthouse itself.

She remembers the Rayleys, seeing the essence of their relationship summed up in pictures of her own invention. She senses the violence of their disagreements, and the loneliness of each, only to be resolved when the sexual strain had gone. The jealousy and competition disappears when Paul finds another woman and he and Minta become just good friends.

Lily feels a certain triumph over Mrs Ramsay. The

Rayleys' marriage, as such, had failed. She and Mr Bankes had not married. Mrs Ramsay is dead and seems lost, unimportant and uninfluential now. 'What was this mania of hers for marriage?' Then she remembers the power and force of Paul Rayley's love; one had to admit the glory of love. She considers her friendship with William Bankes, his understanding, his appreciation of beauty. In her own way, she had loved him; Mrs Ramsay did have 'astonishing power after all'. Lily is perturbed. Life is complex; individual parts are contradictory and do not seem to fit together. She wants to ask Mr Carmichael so much about life, death, Mrs Ramsay.

The drawing room steps are empty; Mrs Ramsay is no longer there. The key to the meaning of life, and therefore of art, lies with her. Lily cries her name aloud. Perhaps the poet can give the answer. All changes, but not words, not paint. Even if her picture is poor, it will remain for ever. Art then is a representation of life, it is the truth and is undying. The values are eternal.

Reaching this conclusion about her picture, Lily weeps at the beauty of the idea. One moment all had seemed transient, another moment one saw eternity. Is this life? There are the tragedies, the despair, the friction, the problems and bitterness of life. But there is the ecstasy too.

Lily 'surfaces' to the present, and sees old Mr Carmichael lying on his chair in the garden. Her thoughts go again to Mrs Ramsay: suddenly she feels that if she and Mr Carmichael were to stand up and shout for her, Mrs Ramsay would return:

'Mrs Ramsay!' she said aloud, 'Mrs Ramsay!' The tears ran down her face. (3,6,209)

the fabric must be clamped together The composition of Lily's picture must be strong and unified.

gazing silently about Lily's art is for her a gateway to the mystery and meaning of life.

one seemed to be on a narrow plank Lily's art is a way of working out individual truth. She can only do it alone; it is difficult. The sea here is an image for time and life.

Their lives appeared to her in a series of scenes Lily composes imaginary scenes which reflect the quality of the Rayleys' relationship, showing Minta's glamour and carelessness, and Paul's anxiety and loneliness.

Rickmansworth A small town in Hertfordshire.

reddish light seemed to burn This is the first of a series of images in which Lily senses the power of Paul Rayley's love. It is like a fire and seems almost pagan in its intensity. It is consuming but magnificent. Lily is glad she has avoided it, though recognizing its splendour.

Raphael Italian Renaissance artist (1483–1520), who painted many pictures of the Madonna.

Hampton Court One of the greatest Royal palaces. Lying on the banks of the Thames, it was built in 1514 by Cardinal Wolsey, who subsequently presented it to Henry VIII.

basking like a creature gorged with existence Mr Carmichael seems fulfilled and satisfied by life.

Words fluttered sideways Lily could not find the right words to express precisely what she felt.

arabesques Flowing lines of decorative, or scroll, work.

a pool of thought ... a blade would be flashed Lily sees reality as a pool from which will flash a moment of penetrating insight.

Could things thrust their hands up Lily is overcome by emotion and feels that parts of life, which she would prefer to encounter only at a distance, reach up and seize her, making her participate.

all was miracle ... into the air The good things of life come unexpectedly; all is hazard and risk.

Section 7

The comment on the fish reminds us of the boat still pursuing its course. We are sharply aware of the link between the 'mutilated body' and the pain of Lily, Mr Ramsay and the others.

Section 8

Lily cries out again to Mrs Ramsay, but nothing happens and her pain increases. She is thankful that no one has heard her. Then she is aware of a 'presence': Mrs Ramsay, 'relieved for a moment of the weight that the world had put on her, staying lightly by her side'. Lily is consoled. She looks out to sea, and her thoughts return to the three on their way to the Lighthouse.

No one had seen her ... annihilation In her
  overwhelming emotion Lily is no longer a watcher, but is
  involved. She is immersed in a sea of sensation, of life.
Piccadilly The most famous of all London thoroughfares,
  generally termed the 'hub of the metropolis', with the
  statue of Eros at its centre.
Standard News A former London newspaper.

Section 9

In the boat they are momentarily becalmed. It seems as if even the journey is echoing the rhythms noted before, the rhythms of the Lighthouse itself. They have been rushing on; now they have almost stopped. James is afraid that his father will grow impatient, in his usual unreasonable manner. He experiences the same deep violent mood he has known as a little boy; but now, like Cam, he becomes conscious of the complexity of his father's personality. He hates his tyranny yet he also sees a sad old man. He will fight the despotism, but how will he respond to the friendliness, the kindness and the excitement, that are also characteristics of his father?

James also realizes that he and his father are alike, and tread the same path through 'a waste of snow and rock very lonely and austere'. He sums up the feeling of terror and anger he has for his father in the image of a wheel crushing someone's foot. The foot is badly hurt but the wheel has been innocent. He explores the idea that this father does not mean to hurt people – it is simply his nature to be utterly himself: true and honest; progressing in a straight line.

Ten years before, his father had disappointed him over the Lighthouse trip. He had associated his father with 'something arid and sharp'; his mother, with leaves, flowers and soft sounds. As a child, the Lighthouse was a 'misty-looking tower with a yellow eye that opened suddenly and softly'. Now, with the passing of the years, James sees it 'stark and straight ... barred with black and white'. On one level these images suggest the romantic, almost magic associations the Lighthouse had for a child, as opposed to the more realistic view of the adolescent. But the image he has as a child seems very feminine, associated strongly with his mother, while the view of the present is more connected with his father. Both images are true. This sums up one of the main themes. The author shows the complexity of people, of relationships, of events.

James thinks about his parents. His mother had appeared to him as the source of all life: between them there was total truth. This is a different kind of truth from the fact-facing of his father; this is the truth of love and understanding. Yet, though he concentrates on his mother, he cannot shake off an awareness of his father.

Slowly, the whole family are moving towards the moment when they will be unified, when they will understand one another.

that fierce sudden black-winged harpy James sees Mr Ramsay's tyranny as a rapacious monster.

the many leaves Past experiences are seen as a forest.

the wheel was innocent James sees that his father is not deliberately brutal.

something arid and sharp descended James remembers how his father obtruded into his happiness as a child, destructively.

he had brought his blade down Mr Ramsay had, in the first Part of the book, injured James's feelings by decreeing that they could not go to the Lighthouse.

conducting some secret symphony Mr Ramsay seems elated and fulfilled by some inner harmony.

Section 10

Lily stands looking out across the bay. It is a beautiful day, for the sea is still and 'stretched like silk across the bay'. The vanished steamer leaves a valedictory scroll of smoke hanging in the air.

they had become part of the nature of things Lily's words emphasize the symbolic journey that is being undertaken, and the acceptance and fulfilment that will come out of it.

Section 11

The boat sails on and Cam senses the adventure. They are escaping now from the island, from the past. They are seeking out the new – the Lighthouse. The tensions have receded, leaving her with feelings of delight. In her new-found happiness she discovers that the island is beautiful. Her thoughts become more positive. She recollects her father's friends as benign, comfortable, contributing to a gentle safe environment. Her father in his study has seemed lovable and wise. As she watches him reading in the boat her heart goes out to him, understanding something of him and his feelings. Instinctively she wants James to watch him too. As her feelings change, so the island becomes small, indistinct. They are a long way out on their journey now.

wheedling a large flock of sheep Cam sees her father once more as the leader of a great expedition, or as a shepherd bringing his flock to safety.

The sea was more important now For Cam, it is the future life that means more now than the island; the past; life and its difficulties.

how we perished Cam, in repeating the lines of the Cowper poem, echoes her father. She is beginning to see what he sees, and feel what he feels, about life.

Section 12

Finding problems with the composition of her picture, Lily concentrates on grasping a concept that is eluding her as she tries to conjure up a complete sense of Mrs Ramsay. At first she feels the 'completeness' of the whole scene, which is the reason for her originally having fallen in love with the place and with the Ramsays. It is her gift to bring together 'those globed compacted things'. It is the gift of the artist. Still her sense of harmony is not yet reflected in her picture. The picture is of the house, Mrs Ramsay and James. Mr Ramsay is still an alien element.

Lily sits down to resolve her problem; watching Mr Carmichael, she goes on to consider the intricacies and difficulties of human relationships. She knows something of Mr Carmichael, but nothing more than an outline.

She returns to thinking of Mrs Ramsay, always so active, her instinct 'turning her infallibly to the human race', while both Lily and Mr Carmichael believe more in the 'supremacy of thought' than action. Diverse personalities can clash and grate, just as she and Charles Tansley had. When she had heard him lecturing in a half empty hall he was, characteristically, condemning, denouncing – and preaching brotherly love. The irony here is obvious. To Lily he seems incongruous, but she remembers how Mrs Ramsay had softened him and seen him in a different light. Ruefully, Lily realizes that our views of people are often false. How then can one know anyone; how can one be unbiased? She reverts to thinking of Mrs Ramsay and her relationship with her husband. Until she can fathom this, Lily's picture will never be finished.

The relationship between Mr and Mrs Ramsay was neither harmonious nor simple; but it had dignity. Prue had been encouraged by her mother to recognize the completeness in marriage that would one day be hers, but it had been, for her, a short happiness. Lily muses on a picture she might have painted, The waves sounding hoarse on the stones, they went, the three of them, with Mrs Ramsay walking quickly in front 'as if expected to meet someone round the corner'. Lily turns the deaths of the three Ramsays into an adventure, a journey.

Suddenly Lily sees someone is at the window casting a shadow over the step. Intrigued, she begins to paint again. She longs to experience the ordinary and, at the same time, to elevate it into a miracle or an ecstasy. Then it seems to her that Mrs Ramsay is there, quietly knitting. This very scene is a miracle, an ecstasy, partly because it gives Lily a moment of insight and partly for what Mrs Ramsay represents – life, and the renewal of life. As the meaning of Mrs Ramsay becomes clear, so Lily needs the other half, too: one is not enough. She looks across the bay for Mr Ramsay; it is not only Mrs Ramsay who is important, but the two together, as individuals and as symbols of the wholeness of life.

puffing and blowing like some sea monster If the sea is life, then Mr Carmichael is at its centre and understands it.

one of those globed, compacted things Lily's picture and her thoughts about the scene bring a unity, form and meaning to the place.

plantains Broad-leaved weeds, often found in lawns.

sitting on the world Lily feels herself at grips with the whole meaning of life.

one would be thinking of Greek temples Lily sees Mrs Ramsay as a Greek goddess.

Golder's Green A district of north-west London.

a whipping-box Someone to blame or criticize.

crinoline A very wide dress worn over a hooped petticoat.

peg-top trousers Breeches.

an echo which chimed in the air Lily is aware of the rhythms of life, of the way emotions are repeated.

the very figure of a famished wolfhound A further image that suggests Mr Ramsay's leanness, fierceness and hardness.

among the pear trees ... raspberry beds A humorous comment, which also suggests the natural fruitful quality of the Ramsays' love.

She had let the flowers fall Lily sees the death of Prue as the loss of one of Mrs Ramsay's flowers.

The hills were austere Lily has a picture of death as a journey into a harsh barren landscape.

Section 13

The boat is approaching the Lighthouse. James looks compassionately at his father, who now seems old. James sees the Lighthouse in its starkness and bareness. It represents truth. He shares his knowledge with his father, and it is a different kind of knowledge from that of the old ladies who talked of niceness and sweetness. The approach of the male to life is very different from that of the female.

To Cam, her father seems like a great bird floating off to some desolate stump. He escapes her and all of them. He cannot be tied down wholly possessed or known. Now the island is far behind, its details lost, but its power still asserting itself. It has meaning; life has gone on here generation after generation.

Mr Ramsay enjoys his communication with the fisherman. Cam feels the rightness of everything and knows she is safe with her father and that he will protect her gallantly. He is leading them on a great expedition, teaching them wisely how to behave, how to live; it is emphasized that Macalister and Ramsay are old – it is the children who will go on.

When Macalister shows them the place where the three sailors drowned, James and Cam wait for their father to shout his poem, but he does not. Now that he is calm he sees it as a natural event. This is symbolic of the change in him. He no longer sees the death of his wife as a great disrupting tragedy, so he has no further need to overreact. It is life. It is natural. Having reached this point Mr Ramsay is able to encourage James, and he praises him for steering so well. This gives James immense pleasure. As they sail on, exhilarated, to the Lighthouse, something positive has been achieved.

As they draw near the Lighthouse Mr Ramsay is completely ready to land. Symbolically, he is reaching fulfilment. He looks back searchingly at the island, while Cam sees only a blur. He can at last leave the past behind; he sees both it and life clearly. He is approaching peace.

In their new relationship with their father Cam and James are happy to give him anything he wants. He has inspired new feelings of warmth in them, he has re-lit the magic of human feeling, responsiveness and inter-dependence. But Mr Ramsay now demands nothing, nor does he need anything. He is alone. He might be thinking, 'I have reached it. I have found it'. To his children he seems young again. James and Cam follow him gladly, in complete contrast to their reluctant gloom earlier.

like some old stone James sees Mr Ramsay as austere, desolate, hard and lonely.

we are driving before a gale Again from *The Castaway*. Like Cam, James too now feels more in tune with his father, and echoes his words.

he floated off ... somewhere far away on some desolate stump An echo of other images used of Mr Ramsay. He was essentially alone, facing the harsh truth about the world.

nothing was left ... across her mind Cam sees the vessel of incense in her imagination, suggesting reverence and perhaps peace. The colour and the rhythm reflect the qualities of the sea itself.

as if he were a great Spanish gentleman Cam sees her father as imbuing simple things with great courtesy and dignity. He is a great man.

tacked Changed direction when sailing to windward.

Section 14

Lily knows they must have reached the Lighthouse. And she is tired: her journey is linked with their journey. She had wanted to give Mr Ramsay sympathy and understanding. She now feels this. She can appreciate him as well as Mrs Ramsay.

Mr Carmichael gets up from his chair to gaze over the bay. He emerges from his own thoughts to echo Lily's. They are both aware of the significance of reaching the Lighthouse, and Lily realizes that he now sees life in true perspective. She returns to her picture, drawing a swift certain line in the centre. It is finished. Her vision is complete. The line may be Mr Ramsay, it may be the Lighthouse, it may be truth – all the images are bound up together. Lily's journey is over. She has at last learned the significance of both Mr and Mrs Ramsay; and her art will express this vision for ever.

an old pagan God Lily sees Mr Carmichael as Neptune (the Roman god of the sea), or Poseidon (his Greek counterpart).

trident The three-pronged sceptre of Neptune or Poseidon.

a wreath of violets Lily sees Mr Carmichael as a god strewing flowers, blessing the world and understanding all things.

Revision questions on Part 3

1 What makes Lily uneasy about her return to the island before the departure of the expedition to the Lighthouse? And what is the general atmosphere?
2 Discuss the significance of the relationship between Lily and Mr Ramsay in Part 3.
3 Show how the children's attitudes to their father gradually change as the Lighthouse is approached.
4 How are the journey to the Lighthouse and the painting of Lily's picture schematically linked?
5 Show how the events of the past are so significant in Part 3.

6 Discuss Lily's attitude to love, and show why her relationship with William Bankes had been so satisfactory to her.

7 In what way does Mr Carmichael play an important part in Part 3?

8 What is the significance of reaching the Lighthouse?

Mrs Ramsay

It was her instinct to go, an instinct like the swallows for the south, the artichokes for the sun, turning her infallibly to the human race, making her nest in its heart. (3,12)

The character of Mrs Ramsay is at the heart of the meaning of the book. She is both an individual character, with all the different facets of her personality viewed from many angles, and she symbolizes some of the good forces in life.

She is shown in many different roles. We see her as a loving and sympathetic mother, concerned about the well-being of her eight children; protecting them, encouraging them and understanding their needs. She is also a practical housewife – anxious about household expenses, worried by the shabbiness of the furniture, exasperated by the untidiness of her family – trying to run her house in an orderly way. As a wife, she loves and understands her husband, supporting him, recognizing his weaknesses but admiring his strength of mind. Although she is often irritated and offended by him – after all, she has a somewhat different outlook on life – she invariably gives him her love, smooths over any difficulties or tensions, and provides the foundations of a truly fruitful and fulfilling marriage. In her role as hostess she tries to make all her guests happy, noticing if they seem ill-at-ease, is concerned and sympathetic towards their problems. At the dinner-party she makes sure that the food will be special, eases the tension between the guests and makes them feel relaxed and content. She tries to help her friends: encouraging Paul and Minta to marry; wondering if she can bring Mr Bankes and Lily Briscoe together. Not content with ministering to her family, friends and acquaintances, she is also interested in the poor and the sick, and is agitated about problems of poverty and hygiene. She is a dispenser of charity as well as of love.

Lily Briscoe thinks that 'Fifty pairs of eyes were not enough to get round that one woman with.' We are not given fifty different viewpoints; but the complexity of Mrs Ramsay's personality is suggested by letting us see her through many different eyes. She is appreciated for various things: Mr Bankes admires her beauty; Charles Tansley is moved to an awareness of her attractions through her sympathy; Lily is aware of the shaping force and influence of her personality; her husband loves her simplicity of mind. But she is also criticized. Mr Carmichael does not trust her and finds her too over-whelmingly organizing; Charles Tansley scorns her ex-aggerations; Mr Bankes is annoyed at her triviality and self-centredness; Lily is irritated by her matchmaking and her attitude to men. And her husband dislikes her disregard of facts and her ability to escape into herself. There are many other examples.

Not only do we see Mrs Ramsay from the outside; we are also taken into her inner self. We are told that she is very beautiful; she is fifty; wears grey and changes into a black dress; is short-sighted; she knits; she exaggerates; she organizes. This allows us to see her clearly in the ordinary world. But there is an inner life too, and this is where we see Mrs Ramsay's real significance, her real self. We see that she is very aware of the sorrows of life, and that, despite her personal happiness, she is pessimistic about the future.

She is sometimes made weary by the burdens of family life and the continual outflow of emotion and sympathy for others – the giving while others take. However, she has the ability to find her own calm, as well as providing it for others. She retreats into a kind of mystical detachment, where the enigmas and mysteries of life are revealed and made clear. Life has a purpose and an order, and these moments give her the strength to continue.

Her success, in the end, brings strength to others. At the close of the book, Lily recognizes her greatness, her creativity, her soothing influence. Whatever she does, Mrs Ramsay creates order, stability and harmony. She is a positive force in life, like an artist shaping events with an intuitive purpose. Her intuition often clashes with Mr Ramsay's insistence on facts. She senses what is the right thing to do and say, what is most positive: she gets to the heart of what people need, what is important and what reality is. For her, reality is not fact but feeling.

Her beauty is important. She is much loved for this. She seems a symbol for the beauty of life, for the feminine principle. She is the symbolic mother; giver of life, producer of children. She encourages marriage in the knowledge that life is good and must go on. Her intuitive knowledge is creative and fertile. Many of the images that surround her are those connected with trees, fruit and flowers, suggesting natural fertility: she is further symbolized by her green shawl; she is the centre of the household; people turn to her. She responds unselfishly with love and sympathy, which bind people together, which create a harmonious community, and which continue to influence others even after death.

Mr Ramsay

It was his fate, his peculiarity, whether he wished it or not, to come out thus on a spit of land which the sea is slowly eating away, and there to stand, like a desolate sea-bird, alone. (1,8)

Mr Ramsay, a well-known philosopher, eleven years older than his wife, is in many ways her opposite. While she is so often tending to other people, he is alone on the terrace or out in the countryside. As she creates harmony and is kind and responsive towards others, he creates tension and is rude, angry, impatient or unsympathetic. The focal point of Mrs Ramsay's life is her family; with him it is his work. And he even feels some resentment of his family, partly blaming them for his failure to produce the great work he had hoped for. He is self-centred and self-pitying; demanding sympathy, love and support. Through the imagery he is presented as hard, masculine and fierce: 'the beak of brass'; 'the arid scimitar'; 'the famished wolfhound'.

Compared with his wife he seems unsympathetic; and he is seen very much more from the outside than she is: he is given few interior monologues; often we merely guess what he is thinking, through the observations of Mrs Ramsay, Lily or the children. However, like all the characters in the novel, Mr Ramsay is not straightforward; one cannot simply dismiss him as a boor. There are contradictory elements in his character; and others respond to him in various ways at different times. Perhaps his family involvement has prevented him from becoming a really great philosopher; but there is a warm simplicity about him, noted by both Lily and William Bankes, which is seen in his enjoyment of dogs, children, the fisherman's company, and in his response to Scott's novels.

Mr Ramsay's philosophy of life is a stern one: he seeks the truth with unwavering purpose and intellectual honesty. For him the facts and predicaments of this world must be faced squarely. He struggles to make progress with his philosophical work, to go beyond 'Q', and this takes him away from the world of his family. He is seen as a kind of hero, the explorer pushing forward into the unknown places – courageous, undaunted, and essentially alone. These qualities of his are admirable; yet his sternness can be crass and inconsiderate. He dashes James's hopes about going to the Lighthouse; his principles are more important to him than his son's feelings.

Although we can see him as heroic, at other times Mr Ramsay appears comic. His self-dramatization leads to such eccentricities as reciting heroic poetry aloud or groaning extravagantly in his misery. For a man dedicated to seeking the truth, he shows an amusing need for admiration and flattery. His major pursuits are intellectual, but he can be mean about money; and he has a great enthusiasm for good boots!

At other times he is pathetic. He wants to be great, but feels a failure. He is proud, aloof, masculine, but needs the love of his wife so much that he is desolated at her death – turning anywhere, even to Lily, for sympathy. He loves his children, but alienates their feelings by his behaviour.

So, just as we see Mrs Ramsay in different roles, we see Mr Ramsay too as philospher, father, husband and friend; in all his different, contradictory moods. For all his weaknesses and his apparent harsh and negative attitudes, there is a way in which he seems complementary to his wife, rather than being totally in opposition. She is (literally) short-sighted and he long-sighted. And (figuratively) they have different ways of looking at life. Mrs Ramsay is an obvious success, but at the end of the book Mr Ramsay succeeds too: he leads his children to the Lighthouse; and Lily realizes that she needs to put him in her picture.

Lily Briscoe

There was in Lily a thread of something: a flare of something; something of her own which Mrs Ramsay liked very much indeed, but no man would, she feared. (1,17)

Although the relationship and personalities of Mr and Mrs Ramsay lie at the centre of the book, much of Part 3 deals with Lily's consciousness, and the way in which she achieves her vision of the *meaning* of Mr and Mrs Ramsay. Her picture sums up the miracle of life.

At the beginning of the book she is thirty-three, and different from the other women, Mrs Ramsay, Minta and Prue. Unlike them, she is not beautiful, and Mrs Ramsay thinks she is unlikely to marry, as men will not be attracted to her. She does not find relationships with men easy to establish, for she is unable to give to them, and thus bolster their egos – as Mrs Ramsay and Minta Doyle are quite ready to do with Mr Ramsay! She does not see her role in life as that of the supportive female, being angry with herself for her own insincerity when she is kind to Charles Tansley at the dinner-table. And she is quite unable to give the easy sympathy that Mr Ramsay demands of her after his wife's death.

Lily seems virginal, shy, and nervous of men. She is appalled by Mr Ramsay's insistent masculinity, and contemptuous and angry at Charles Tansley's claim for the superiority of men. She sees that Tansley needs to believe in it, that it upholds his male arrogance. Because she is obviously not the natural wife and mother that the other three women are, Lily is irritated and amused by Mrs Ramsay's hopes for her (Lily's) marriage. She does not feel that this is at all necessary for her own fulfilment, which lies in her art. Mrs Ramsay (see 1,17), fears that Lily may never marry, but feels that an older man like William Bankes would be a suitable husband for Lily.

Nevertheless, she is fascinated by Mrs Ramsay, love and marriage. She is aware of Mrs Ramsay's happiness, her full satisfaction, and she will remember for ever the blaze of Paul Rayley's love, though she feels that she herself would be scorched or dissolved by such a force. She is really an onlooker at life, withdrawn and aloof from its forces and turbulence, yet critically aware of what is going on around her. She loves Mrs Ramsay, missing her greatly when she is dead, responding to her as one creative artist to another. She senses the other woman's goodness, her position at the heart of life; and she recognizes her own insignificance by comparison. She also admires the greatness of Mr Ramsay's mind, makes allowances for his behaviour – aware that, in a sense, he lives in another world.

Lily is the artist: her role in life is not that of the wife, the mother. It is rather that of standing back, viewing in proportion and perspective the scenes around her, then fashioning them into an harmonious whole, interpreting and presenting them to the world and to posterity. Although she knows she is not a good artist, Lily finds fulfilment in her art and is determined to retain her freedom to paint. In moments of stress, at the dinner-table, she returns to thinking about her picture: that is her happiness and satisfaction. Mrs Ramsay admires her; she senses that though Lily is not so beautiful as Minta, at forty she will be better.

She has an independence that is admirable, not to most men certainly, but which is perhaps appreciated by Mr Bankes. In fact with Mr Bankes, the elderly widower, Lily feels at ease; she does not mind his seeing her picture, and she admires his scientific disinterest. He does not demand anything of her, he does not try to crush her; he treats her as an intelligent human being, not just as a female. Their platonic friendship is a pleasure to Lily; in her calm way she loves him, but it is an asexual love. She loves the Ramsays too, with their children and household – quite fiercely at times. It is a full emotional response to their goodness and the quality of their life.

Lily naturally tends to visualize abstract concepts, to see them in pictures, and she also tends to see certain scenes in a symbolic way. She sees Mr Ramsay's work as a kitchen table (an image suggested to her by his son Andrew). In observing the Ramsay family playing ball in the garden, she sees it as a symbol of harmony, of marriage. As she paints her picture in Part 3, her mind is continually ranging over past experiences; putting things together, comparing, contrasting and making sense out of events. At last, this leads to her finishing the picture – all her feelings, experience and awareness of what the Ramsays represent have gone into it.

William Bankes

a botanist, a widower, smelling of soap, very scrupulous and clean (1,4)

He is an elderly botanist, a widower with no children. His friendship with Mr Ramsay is a long-standing one, though they see each other only intermittently, having drifted apart a little since Mr Ramsay's marriage. Rather like Lily, Bankes remains on the sidelines of the Ramsay household. He comes to dinner with them reluctantly, merely for the sake of pleasing Mrs Ramsay, whose beauty and moral purity he has long admired; he feels he would be better employed at his work. He seems a little crusty, dried up: children do not respond to him; he is pernickety about his food; self-satisfied about the organization of his own life, smug that he does not live in as chaotic an atmosphere as do the Ramsays.

Lily sees Bankes as a great man, a typical scientist. She admires his aloofness, his disinterest, his unemotional approach to life. She believes that, in his feeling for Mrs Ramsay, he appreciates beauty in a purely aesthetic way. But Mrs Ramsay pities him. She senses his loneliness, his envy of the family group's liveliness, his sorrow at having no children. She responds to him as a man. It is interesting to compare him with his friends. He does not have the warmth and humanity of Mr Ramsay, merely perfect courtesy; neither does he have Lily's creativeness. Like all the characters in the book, he is presented as complex: both smug and doubting, certain and unsure; satisfied and lonely; dried up and kind.

Charles Tansley

put them all on edge somehow with his acid way of peeling the flesh and blood off everything (1,1)

He is a protégé of Mr Ramsay, and behaves in a sycophantic way towards him, admiring him yet really out to better himself through the connection. He is a dry, scholarly intellectual who is seeking academic fame; he is writing a dissertation, and by the end of the novel he has succeeded in gaining a fellowship.

The rest of the Ramsay family, particularly the children, dislike Tansley. He is arrogant and assertive, always twisting conversations, either to centre them on himself or to disparage the ideas of others and thus demonstrate his own superiority. At the dinner party he seethes with frustration because he is not the focus of attention, and in this mood he becomes hypersensitive, aware that he is not in the right clothes and thinking that everyone is laughing at him. He is awkward, conscious of his social inferiority, and is abrupt and rude – in contrast to the urbane, polished manners of William Bankes, who is also feeling frustrated. When he is made to feel lacking in any way, Tansley's feelings become violent. He has enormous pride in himself, and is determined to outdo everyone else. His sneering at women's ways and achievements stems from his obsessive need to feel superior.

Mrs Ramsay is the one who takes the trouble to talk to Tansley and discover his background; he had suffered poverty in his childhood, his father having been a chemist and his grandfather a fisherman. From the age of thirteen he had worked his own way up, winning scholarships and living frugally. We notice his resentment of the middle classes; his concentration upon academic brilliance; his disdain of material possessions; his ruthless egotism. All these spring from his feelings of humiliation at being poor'

Although one might sympathize with Tansley and pity him, as Mrs Ramsay does; and recognize his fine intelligence and the fact that he is well-informed, as Mr Bankes does; nevertheless the fact remains that he is an unsympathetic character. When Lily has listened to his

lecture in the half empty hall, all she can remember is
that he has been denouncing someone. He has married
and achieved the success he craved, but as a person he
remains corrosive, abrasive. But he does have his one
selfless moment, and this is brought about by Mrs Ramsay: he is so moved by her beauty and her sympathy as to
forget himself for a moment and feel pride in her company; she manages to initiate a warm outgoing feeling,
even in Tansley.

Augustus Carmichael

He was an inscrutable old man, with the yellow stain on his
beard, and his poetry, and his puzzles, sailing serenely
through a world which satisfied all his wants (3,6)

He is an old friend of Mr Ramsay, a poet who eventually
finds success. Mrs Ramsay feels sorry for him, as she
thinks that an unfortunate marriage has blighted his life
and caused him to mistrust women. He is the one man in
the book who hardly responds to Mrs Ramsay at all, is
apparently unmoved by her beauty, and regards her
kindness with irony – possibly seeing it spring from self-
centredness. He does not need her attention and help. He
seems to live in a world of his own; taking opium; sitting
by himself on the lawn; reading in his room late into the
night; asking for nothing. Although he has had tragedy
in his life (the death of Andrew particularly pained him)
there is a serenity about him that Lily likes. He too seems
to be an onlooker; and as a poet he is a thinker rather
than a man of action. In the end, Augustus Carmichael is
almost like a figure of fate, looking upon the events of life
with detachment; not with blind indifference, but with
acceptance and compassion.

Minta Doyle

She wore her golden haze (1,17)

Minta Doyle and Paul Rayley are important in that they reflect the influence of Mrs Ramsay. Their engagement is her success, as she has partly manipulated them and encouraged them to marry, believing this to be the best way of life. Minta is essentially feminine, being beautiful with a special glow, a lustre that is attractive to men; and she knows how to charm. Full of life and exuberance, she is a little wild, perhaps irresponsible, and it may be her fault that the marriage is not a success. She is presented in the book as a contrast to Lily; physically more blooming, but without her mental reserves and independence.

Paul Rayley

He turned on her cheek the heat of love, its horror, its cruelty, its unscrupulosity (1,17)

Paul contrasts with the other men in the book. He is not an intellectual, not 'dried up', and Mrs Ramsay likes his simplicity and his good looks. His love for Minta is a powerful force that launches him on the excitements of life. Mrs Ramsay is impressed; Lily is fascinated and overawed by this force; and everyone at the dinner table is aware of it. However, this great love is eventually to fade to mere friendship as their marriage breaks up and he finds another, more serious woman.

The children

James is the Ramsays' youngest child, six at the opening of the book and sixteen at the end. As a child he is sensitive and emotional, quick to feel sorrow or joy. He has a close, loving relationship with his mother, who is the centre of his life; and he resents his father, who takes away his mother's attention and quashes his ideas. In the last part of the book he has come to terms with his feelings for his father: he is determined to resist his tyranny, while he has a growing awareness of the fineness of his father's courage, rectitude and nobility. In the end he turns out to be very like Mr Ramsay – stern and moral, outwardly unbending and essentially alone, yet responding to warmth and praise. Upright and clear sighted, he too needs love.

Cam at seven is a wild and fierce little girl, upsetting Mr Bankes by not responding to him. At the end of the book, in the boat, she is, like James, suddenly drawn to her father. She too has hated his tyranny, hated his insistence upon the memories of dead people from the past; and she wanted to be free. But she is feminine: she has a certain vagueness of mind – facts are not important – and she is softened by her father's friendliness and teasing. She has the sense of his being a protector, a leader, a gallant gentleman.

The other children, *Andrew, Prue, Nancy, Rose, Jasper* and *Roger*, are not differentiated in any great detail. Andrew is intellectual, brilliant at mathematics (perhaps like his father), and is later to die in the war in France. Prue is beautiful, marries young and seems destined to be like her mother, but she dies tragically in childbirth. Nancy seems imaginative, is at an age when she is beginning to wonder about life, but young enough to be embarrassed by love. Rose is creative (Mrs Ramsay thinks) and highly sensitive, and will one day suffer. Jasper likes shooting, and is impatient with his mother's sentimentality.

Mrs McNab is the old caretaker who looks after the house in Scotland. She is a grotesque comic figure, battling against the ravages of time. Although she is decrepit and witless, her memories of the Ramsay family remain fresh – they have not decayed like the house – and, with persistence and an indomitable spirit, she struggles to do her work. She seems to represent the human ability to soldier on, to find enjoyment in life, despite all its difficulties and tragedies.

Themes and symbolism

Themes

The individual and the nature of life

Because of the structure of the book, based on the interior monologue, what is particularly emphasized is the consciousness of the individual. This awareness is intricate, free to wander where it will, across the dimensions of time, through material barriers, drifting from one thing to another. But we see that though the mind appears to act in a random way, there is an underlying pattern, and it seeks to unify its own experiences and images, arranging them, reworking them, and trying to make sense of them. Each individual struggles to find a sense of purpose in a world that is shifting, seeking to discover what is significant from a myriad of experiences, and, above all, the meaning of their own identity.

Each is aware of the shortness of this life, the impersonality of time, fortune and death, and tries to impose a harmony on what seems chaotic. Essentially this pursuit is a lonely one. There is the comfort of love, marriage, friendships and children, all of which need a creative response to flourish and provide joy; but finally the individual must work out his fate alone. Mrs Ramsay in her more mystical moments, cut off from domestic pressures, senses that the reality of life is something private. All superficialities are cast off, one shrank 'to being oneself, a wedge-shaped core of darkness, something invisible to others'. Reduced to mere consciousness, there is a sense of peace and harmony, of seeing into the life of things, of being part of some huge pattern. Mr Ramsay, too, faces basic reality by himself, 'to come out thus on a spit of land which the sea is slowly eating away, and there to stand like a desolate sea-bird, alone'. His vision is bleak, but he has the satisfaction of its being the truth.

What is life? What is the point of life? What is it worth? These are some of the questions the author is seeking to answer. In her own life Virginia Woolf experienced the joy and exhilaration of creative activity; was intensely receptive to beauty and the complexity of life; and had a happy marriage. But she also went through agonies of depression and lack of confidence; sensed her life to be a failure; felt increasingly alone and a burden on her family; and eventually committed suicide. These extremes of experience, this ambivalence and polarity of life, are expressed in *To the Lighthouse*.

Life can seem totally chaotic and disharmonious, and based on the random principle of fate. But what the author shows us in *To the Lighthouse* is that there is an underlying pattern to life, a unity that makes sense. The symbol of the Lighthouse itself reflects this. It has a rhythm of light and dark; it stands firm on a little rock surrounded by the dashing sea; it is stable in a changing world. Nature too has the rhythm of light and dark; ripeness changes to decay; the sea is calm and peaceful or fierce and menacing as it ebbs and flows; animals and plants are fertile and can be organized by man, but some are invasive and destructive. Above all, time has a natural flow from day to night, from summer to winter. With this natural repetition comes a sense of purpose. There is always rebirth: nature rises up again in the spring; humanity will go on; hurt will fade with the onset of new happiness. The transience of one little life is blurred by the knowledge of the permanence of this world. The decay of the house and the deaths of the Ramsays are followed by the reorganizing energy of Mrs McNab and the visit to the Lighthouse by the younger generation.

Virginia Woolf not only sees natural life and the events of fate and time falling into a regular design; she sees the innate qualities of people as also being patterned. All through the book there are significant contrasts in temperament, outlook and reaction. There are the opposing ideas of age and youth; parent and child; husband and wife: but the two most important differences of view seem to lie between the male and the female; the scientific mind and the artistic one.

Mrs Ramsay is the symbol of the feminine: she produces children; loves and is loved; is the centre of human warmth; radiates kindness and delves deep into the backgrounds of other people in an effort to understand; she creates life and harmony. Her way of approaching life is intuitive; she senses what her husband, children and friends need. She will lie if necessary and she will exaggerate, but she will know what is right; she will reach the still centre of things. Mr Ramsay is the intellectual. He reaches the truth by deductive thought, by insistence upon facts and the external reality. He is male: hard, stern, alone, unflinching and unyielding. Thus the two present opposite outlooks on life – but which is right? It seems in the book that Mrs Ramsay's intuitive response is right. We feel that it is good when she tells James that they must go to the Lighthouse, and when she encourages Minta and Paul to marry, even if future events prove her optimism wrong. But that does not mean that of necessity Mr Ramsay is totally wrong. His is simply another way of looking at life – facts have to be faced at some point, and his courage does take the family to the Lighthouse in the end.

So the theme here is that there are two kinds of truth,

perhaps two ways of approaching reality: the feminine way of feeling, perceiving through emotion; and the masculine directness that is sternly intellectual. Perhaps both are necessary. Certainly the more artistic characters, such as Lily, have both outlooks.

Andrew had told Lily that his father's work consisted of 'Subject and object and the nature of reality'. The feminine, intuitive view of life is essentially subjective; the intellectual and scientific is more objective. The views are part of the pattern of human life, and it is the function of the artist to perceive and appreciate both, as Lily and Mrs Carmichael do.

Time

Virginia Woolf's awareness of the passing of time, of the changes it brings, of its inevitability and its indifference to human endeavours, is at the centre of the novel. She knows that the present is evanescent; it slips away, and all too quickly becomes memory. The future is unknown, but decay, loss and death are unavoidable. The past may be safe and unchanging, but our perceptions of it may alter, thus putting it into different perspective. Life, then, is always in a state of flux: nothing seems stable. Joy turns to sorrow; youth to age; fame to anonymity; love to indifference. But human beings seek order and stability: they seek to make sense of the contradictory elements of life; to hold on to the joys they have experienced; they have an instinct to go on living despite tragedy. In *To the Lighthouse*, Virginia Woolf examines the effects of time; deals with different characters' reactions to these effects, and in the end shows a positive way of accepting change.

The three-part structure of the book is in itself a reflection of time. The first part is set on a late summer evening; the second part is night, but a night which is expanded to ten dark years; the third part is morning again. The rhythm here of day, night; summer, winter; light, dark; is symbolic of the flow of life itself in all its vicissitudes.

In the first part of the book we see a happy family, with Mrs Ramsay's love and harmonizing influence at the centre of it. There are many possibilities: Andrew will be a brilliant mathematician; Prue will be a beauty and marry; James will be a judge; Paul and Minta are radiantly in love and marriage lies ahead; Mr Ramsay's work has been brilliant (he has reached 'Q' in his work – will he go on to 'R'?). However, even here there are doubts. Mr Ramsay thinks his work will be forgotten. Mrs Ramsay wishes that her children did not have to grow up and suffer. Both know that time will bring unhappiness.

In the second part 'Time Passes', in the poetic description of the forces of darkness and of the chaos caused by invading nature in the Scottish house, the worst elements of life are presented. Mrs Ramsay, Andrew and Prue die, but their deaths seem insignificant – all the major events of this section are dealt with in parenthesis. The author seems to feel that, compared with the vastness of eternity, an individual's life is tiny and meaningless.

After the idyllic summer of the first part comes war, itself (like time) destructive and indifferent to the human lot. The inroads made on the house are symbolic of the decay of material things and the basic hostility of nature to man's manufactured objects. Time seems to have destroyed so much that was good.

But just as day comes after night, so life has its rhythms too. There is a re-birth, symbolized by the restoration of the house. In the third part of the book, the Ramsay family get to the Lighthouse after all; Mr Ramsay finds something to live for, and the children are united with him in a new feeling of communion. Lily's picture is finished; life goes on. Past events no longer seem so tragic. Mrs Ramsay's influence lives on in people's minds, in Lily's art and the lives of her children. Human hope and determination are renewed: individuals may be gone, but their values, spirit and strengths are eternal. They are part of the pattern of time as a whole.

There is also another way in which Virginia Woolf uses time, and this is in the development of the personalities of her characters. In the freedom of their own thoughts, people are able to go at will from past to present; something in the present will turn the mind to past events. People do not think chronologically, and images of the past are often more significant than present ones, particularly if they are connected with a strong emotion. It is Lily in particular who ranges over past events, seeking to find order, to explore and to bring meaning to the present and, in her art, to the future.

Art

As a writer, Virginia Woolf must make sense of life, convey its reality, organize, select, and fashion material so as to create a cohesive and coherent whole. Life is fragmented and contradictory. It is transitory, the life of an individual soon being over; it can be lonely and splintered, each person always essentially cut off from others. In *To the Lighthouse* Lily, the artist, is the one who must shape life. From the start she is concerned about the composition of her picture: it must have harmony, balance and unity. But it is not just a matter of technical precision: there must be an understanding of the subject, an emotional response to it; and the creative ability to select the right elements.

For Lily it is Mrs Ramsay who seems to hold the key to life. Mrs Ramsay herself is creative: she brings warmth and harmony to events. She encourages love and friendship; she is beautiful and wise and knows by intuition what is right and good. Lily wishes that she and Mrs Ramsay could be one. She desires unity, complete understanding; she wishes she could 'unseal' Mrs Ramsay, but this is impossible.

Lily does finally get her vision of Mrs Ramsay and finishes the picture. But before that, she has had to understand, to react in sympathy, to feel in harmony with the people and the place. She has seen Mrs Ramsay in a loving relationship with her children; she has felt a love for the whole family and for the house by the sea. She has at last reacted with sympathy towards Mr Ramsay, and recognized the importance of his journey to the Lighthouse; and she has got the past into perspective. In other words, she has herself created harmony. She has fashioned meaning out of her own experiences and observations, and this meaning is transferred to her art.

Lily realizes that Mrs Ramsay's creative talents made her an artist in her own way. She created moments that lasted and survived like works of art. She was able to say 'Lily stand still here'. In art, one not only expresses elements of life in a unified way, one also 'makes of the moment something permanent'. Although, after the death of Mrs Ramsay's friends and family, her influence and significance will be forgotten, it will live on in Lily's picture. Therefore art not only reflects the stable and unchanging elements of life, it is itself permanent: art is life.

However, there is no permanent, perfect harmony: there are only moments of bliss in a dark world. Mrs Ramsay is not successful in her efforts to bring people together; and Lily knows herself to be an indifferent painter: her picture will probably be rolled up or hung in an attic. One can only try to create order out of disorder, harmony out of discord. Mr Bankes and Mr Ramsay do it through their work, one solving scientific problems, the other reducing the meaning of life to the letters of the alphabet and working through them. Lily and Mr Carmichael do it through their pictures and poetry.

Literature plays an important part in the events of the book. Mr Ramsay is given to quoting lines of verse in moments of excitement. The end of the dinner-party is summed up by a poem. When Mr and Mrs Ramsay are sitting together reading, he becomes engrossed in a Scott novel, she in a Shakespearean sonnet; later Mrs Ramsay reads one of Grimm's fairy tales to their son James. There is a sense here of a fusion of art and life. The words that are read or recited aloud often reflect the mood of the reader or bear on his consciousness in a special way, making him more alert to his own situation. They highlight his awareness, make it more poignant, more meaningful; emphasizing the harmonies of life, the eternal qualities. Mr and Mrs Ramsay react to the truth and beauty of the words they read, and this, in turn, leads to their renewed sense of joy in their love for each other. Here, art both mirrors life and truly creates it.

Symbolism

The whole structure of the book is based on symbolism: in the first part the window is where people look out and look in, just as the author shows us the thoughts of Mrs

Ramsay as she looks out, and of the others who look in at her. And we see all the characters from both outside and inside.

In Part 2 the night is symbolic of tragedy, and of the forces of chaos and fate. Part 3 focuses on the main symbol of the book; the journey to the Lighthouse, which is at last successfully completed. Note also that just as there are three parts to the book, there are three strokes from the Lighthouse beam.

Apart from the symbolism of the book's structure, Virginia Woolf uses private symbols to expand for us the consciousness of the characters. Just as the characters cannot be totally defined, but only partly perceived or sensed, so her symbols work in the same way. The same symbol may mean different things to different people; the individuals themselves are not wholly aware of the meaning of these, but respond in an emotional way to their significance. The symbolism often highlights a particular moment of happiness, deep feeling, thought, or understanding, but it is itself only vaguely definable. Remember that the author says 'Nothing was simply one thing.'

The Lighthouse

As a child, James sees the Lighthouse as a 'silvery, misty looking tower with a yellow eye that opened suddenly and softly in the evening'. Ten years later he sees it 'stark and straight ... barred with black and white'. He recognizes that both images are true. Just as Mrs Ramsay represents beauty, softness, femininity and intuitive feeling, and Mr Ramsay hardness, courage and the toughness of the intellect, so the Lighthouse can be seen to symbolize both. It shines out in a dark world; it has a regular stroke, creating harmony in the disordered elements; the rock it stands on is a stable point in a turbulent sea. It is beautiful; it is a focal point; it is like Mrs Ramsay. She identifies herself with the 'long steady stroke', and the beauty of it as it 'silvered the rough waves a little more brightly' brings her to a moment of ecstasy when the fulfilling experience of life is made clear to her. It represents the true values of life: its continuance, its harmony; its beauty. Mrs Ramsay has found the truth, and says 'It is enough.'

But Mrs Ramsay is also aware of the Lighthouse being stern, pitiless and remorseless. The truths of life are hard to accept; Mr Ramsay does courageously accept them, standing alone rather like the Lighthouse. His intelligence shines out, 'facing the dark of human ignorance'. So the Lighthouse symbolizes both the beauty and the harshness of this world, reflected in its pattern of light and darkness. It can guide us through the dark, but it cannot change the dark itself. It is aloof: it shines impersonally on to the Ramsays' house during the summer of happiness and the winters of decay.

In the end, it seems to stand as a symbol of life itself. Mrs Ramsay forgets the problems of her own fate and concentrates only upon the light. Mr Ramsay leaves his past anguish behind him and makes true contact with his children on the journey to the Lighthouse. And the rhythms of life, the beauty of life, the truth, are all equated with the lighthouse beam; it represents order.

The book begins with Mrs Ramsay telling James that they will go to the Lighthouse the following day; it ends with Lily's vision, which only comes when she is aware that the Lighthouse has been reached. In a sense, then, the book is about a journey (as, of course, is its title) – a quest that is troublesome and difficult. Mr and Mrs

Ramsay achieve their destinations; and, in their different ways, they prepare their children for the journey.

The sea

In her diary Virginia Woolf wrote, 'But while I write, I am making up "To the Lighthouse" – the sea is to be heard all through it – '.

Like the lighthouse beam, the sea has a rhythm, an ebb and flow. In the book it serves as a perpetual backdrop to the action: on the island they can always hear the sea; they are surrounded by the sea. It is a symbol of time, of eternity, and of the changing nature of life, its joy and sorrow. Mrs Ramsay is sometimes aware of the sound of the waves as a 'measured and soothing tattoo' which she feels is protecting her. The muddle of an individual life is played out against the great pattern of the eternity of time and the renewal of the round of existence. Though the waves are separate, they form a unified whole. On the other hand she also realizes a 'ghostly roll of drums remorsely beat the measure of life, made one think of the destruction of the island and its engulfment in the sea.' The sea is an image for the contradictions, the oppositions of life.

Mr Ramsay too is aware of the destructive nature of the sea; it 'eats away the ground we stand on'. He sees that on the voyage of life 'our frail barks founder in the darkness'. Nevertheless he enjoys fighting against it. He loves the fishermen's stories of men 'pitting muscle and brain against the waves and the wind'. He prefers the land to the sea, 'the sandhills dwindling away into darkness'. His mind is turned to facts, his philosophy: things that cannot change and will live on. Nevertheless he is aware that his work might not endure. He has to come to terms with the sea; the poetry that he quotes shows his awareness of the struggle.

In the final part of the book the sea is calm after the storms; on the trip to the Lighthouse the Ramsays slowly come together. The beauty and life of the sea cause a change; and Mr Ramsay realizes that 'the depths of the sea ... are only water after all.' The Lighthouse is reached.

As with the other symbols, the sea does not here represent only one thing: it underlines, harmonizes with and extends a whole range of suggestions. Many of the characters become keenly conscious of the sea, are drawn to it and interpret its meaning in different ways, just as people interpret life in different ways.

The island, the dinner-party, Lily's painting

The *island setting* is used symbolically, emphasizing the isolated nature of the individual's struggle and the smallness of man's life set against eternity. To Cam, however, seated in the boat and seeing the island fade away, it seems to represent the ties of the past. The Lighthouse stands on another tiny island, a still point in the flux of existence. The sand dunes, which Mr Ramsay loves and Mr Bankes associates with his friendship for him, seem connected with external reality, solidarity; a factual truth compared with the more spiritual truth of the sea.

The *dinner-party* is symbolic of the way Mrs Ramsay creates order. She brings everyone together. Her 'Boeuf en Daube' symbolizes life-giving sustenance; it is a ceremonial gift of plenty, celebrating human relationships, love and marriage. She sees the bowl of fruit as a cornucopia of life, 'a trophy fetched from the bottom of the sea'.

Art has already been discussed (see *Themes*, p. 101); but *Lily's painting* symbolizes the way in which life can be crystallized by art. The picture captures for eternity something of human significance. It has the essential balance that has been noted about the form of the book as a whole. It contains the male and the female symbols; it has been painted with both detachment and emotion, joy and sorrow. It sums life up.

Style

All Virginia Woolf's books were written with immense care. She wrote and rewrote and worked certain passages over and over again until she got as near as she could to the effects that she wanted. She was often in despair at the imperfection of her work, extremely sensitive to any criticism, because so much of herself went into her writing, leaving her emotionally drained. Her writing is, in a way, intensely feminine, as she would herself have recognized. It is romantic and imaginative, based on sensibility and feeling. It conveys emotion lyrically and impressionistically through the brilliance, largely reiterative, of symbolic images. Above all, whatever her subject, the author – through the tone, colour, light and shade, radiant elegance of metaphor and description – creates memorable and beautiful pictures that make an aesthetic appeal to the senses.

Her style is essentially poetic. We have noted (p. 16) that she felt *To the Lighthouse* was a kind of elegy; and her husband Leonard referred to it as 'a psychological poem'. Like poetry, her writing has a special intensity and impact: based on metaphor and symbolism, it leads to the fusion of impressions that are solid yet abstract, vivid and philosophical. We are given a very real picture of place and character, but the language moves in such an associative way, building up imagery and symbol, that we are given the sense of a deeper meaning, a strongly aesthetic awareness of the beauty and pathos of life. In her diary Virginia Woolf says of *To the Lighthouse* that it is a 'hard, muscular book'. By this she does not mean it is rational, intellectual and forceful, but that it is structured, highly-wrought and intense. But at another point in her diary she feels that the book is 'soft and pliable'. Because it is impressionistic, it is open to different interpretations and responses, all of which may be equally valid. It is fluid, moving from character to character, from idea to idea.

Her descriptions are often lyrical, as when she writes of the effects of the lighthouse beam on Mrs Ramsay (Part 1, Section 11, hereafter 1, 11), where we are made aware of the colour, the softness, the murmur of the sea and the beauty of the light. The attentive reader will note that this creates a vivid impression of the beauty of the light upon the sea and in the room. As Mrs Ramsay reacts to the light it becomes, in fact, personified: it strokes, hypnotizes, has fingers; it becomes more than just a light. It is symbolic of a greater force; it has power. The image of the sea breaking upon the beach becomes fused with the moment of ecstasy breaking and flooding Mrs Ramsay's mind, giving her a sense of fulfilment and joy. The sea is real; it is rough, it curves and swells and breaks on the beach, but in its association with the steady beauty of the light and Mrs Ramsay's realization of happiness, it too becomes symbolic. Much of Virginia Woolf's writing works in this way; description of external beauty fuses with inner meaning or philosophy.

The descriptions of night and darkness in 'Time Passes' are both pictorial and metaphorical, the pictures and images working together to form a pattern of imagery, a pattern that becomes a symbol of the beauty of life. Look at the passage 2,3, which begins with the words 'But what after all is one night? A short space, especially when the darkness dims so soon'. Read it closely, and you will note that the images of dawn, the renewing of light and life, the birdsong, the green leaf or wave are lost in the long nights of winter. Winter is personified, a figure of fate, reinforced by the idea of the pack of cards.

Here the personification is again symbolic. Winter is representative of the gloomy side of life, the sorrow, but there is light even in winter. The series of images of light in darkness accumulates and in the end symbolizes man's joy in a hostile world. The individual pictures are striking and vivid – 'the plates of brightness', 'the flash of tattered flags kindling', 'the gold letters on marble pages', the bones that 'bleach and burn'. There is a sense of clarity, of brightness, and finally of colour in the gleam of 'yellow moonlight' and the wave 'lapping blue'. As the images become more poetic, so the writing becomes more explicit. The light softens harsh labour, smooths rough stubble and turns the sea to mildness and calm.

There are strong rhythms to Virginia Woolf's prose. She uses short sentences against long; the clauses build up, balance, and reach a climax. She uses contrast and antithesis to enhance these rhythms. She tends to feel her way towards the final effect: image is placed on image; there is a fluidity of description; a measured progress towards exactness, towards the expression of the significance of experience. Her style does not change to differentiate individual characters; they all think in the same poetic, metaphorical way. But her style does change when she wants to indicate a shift of mood. Consider Lily Briscoe, disturbed by her own thoughts towards the end of the book (3,6): the exclamation 'Oh yes!' inserted into the statement reflects emotion; and the accumulation of short sentences suggests the feverishness and fervency of her feelings as she seeks to control and understand them. The questions mount up, become more metaphorical until the climax of the last one is reached: the possibility that life is composed of miracles and dangerous leaps. Here the form of the writing reflects clearly the state of the character's feelings.

Because Virginia Woolf feels that to find the essence of life, one needs to probe inner rather than external realities, she concentrates on the workings of people's minds. Direct speech is desultory and dialogue intermittent – often used merely as a framework within which to set the character's contemplations. And major external events like deaths (and even minor happenings that intrude upon the character's consciousness, as, for example, the squeak of a hinge), are often narrated in parenthesis, as if these are not the things that really matter.

Despite the fact that all her characters appear to think in the same way, they are separated and made distinct by the clusters of metaphors and related images that surround them. Charles Tansley 'put them all on edge somehow with his acid way of peeling the flesh and blood off everything'. He is harsh and abrasive. The intuitive imagination of Mrs Ramsay is summed up in 'Her singleness of mind made her drop plumb like a stone, alight exact as a bird, gave her, naturally this swoop and fall of the spirit upon truth.' It was the fate of Mr Ramsay 'to come out thus on a spit of land which the sea is slowly eating away, and there to stand like a desolate sea-bird, alone'. The author expresses herself most lucidly through the association of different images, and there is a cumulative effect of this that gives the book its special illuminated quality.

Although she is essentially a serious writer, dealing with serious themes, the author does not lack a sense of proportion, a sense of humour. She uses anti-climax to suggest the absurdity of human behaviour: Lily's appalled resistance to Mr Ramsay's overbearing demands upon her sympathy is humorously dealt with, culminating in Lily's outburst and his response over his boots. Mrs McNab is a comic character, rolling and lurching her way through life. Lily's vision of the kitchen table as the symbol of Mr Ramsay's mind shows appreciative irony at the too literal application of the artistic imagination: absurdly, Lily sometimes sees the table resting in a pear tree. Mrs Ramsay's thought: 'she is marrying a man who has a gold watch in a wash-leather bag' reflects the oddity and obliqueness of the mind. There is, throughout the book, a gentle irony and humour at people's idiosyncratic and sometimes egotistical reactions. Charles Tansley 'felt the wind and the cyclamen and the violets for he was walking with a beautiful woman for the first time in his life. He had hold of her bag.' There is both pathos and bathos here as the author shows the significance of a moment that is at the same time trivial. Mr Ramsay's reciting poetry aloud is eccentrically comic, and the writer is at once sympathetic and quizzical over the dramatizing of strong emotion. She feels with her characters but is able to distance them at the same time – in other words, she sees both subjectively and objectively:

Mr Tansley raised a hammer: swung it high in the air; but realizing, as it descended, that he could not smite that butterfly with such an instrument as this, said only that he had never been sick in his life. (1,17).

The hammer metaphor suggests the violence of his emotion, but the anti-climax of his reply reflects the ironic way in which Virginia Woolf views the conventions of social gatherings and traditional attitudes to women.

To sum up, Virginia Woolf, in her poetic descriptions, achieves both immediacy and distance. The interior monologue takes us right into the minds of her characters; the figurative style gives us vivid pictures; the expansion of time gives the effect, the feel of ordinary life. On the other hand, the characters are presented in the third person, which makes them more objective; the use of symbolism, gives a universality to the scenes, makes them less individual; and the underlying irony suggests a detached viewpoint. Just as the main characters, Mr and Mrs Ramsay, reflect the opposite views of intellectual objectivencss and imaginative subjectiveness, so the author embraces both modes in her own style.

General questions and sample answer in note form

1 Virginia Woolf wanted a new name for her type of novel and thought of 'elegy'. How far does *To the Lighthouse* differ from the conventional novel, and do you consider 'elegy' would have been a suitable title?

2 If it is a novel about human relationships, what are the virtues and positive elements that the author sees in these relationships?

3 Virginia Woolf sees that it is impossible to know another human being completely. Discuss the failures of communication that occur in the novel, and discuss their significance.

4 How far do you see the novel as reflecting the differences between masculine and feminine?

5 'How did one judge people, think of them?' Lily wondered. Show how Virginia Woolf expresses this theme in *To the Lighthouse*.

6 How does the author imply that there is a pattern of meaning in the seemingly haphazard and random existence of man?

7 Do you find Mr Ramsay merely cantankerous, negative and tyrannical; or is there any way in which he seems more sympathetic or positive?

8 Show how Lily Briscoe and Mrs Ramsay are both creative in their different ways.

9 What does Virginia Woolf see as the function of the artist in society? Relate your answer carefully to the novel.

10 We are taken into the consciousness of many of the

characters in the book. How far do you find this an
effective technique?

11 Discuss the significance that the author thinks love
has, and show in what different forms it works in the
book.

12 Analyse the different ways in which the author
suggests the constant presence of the sea, and show
their significance.

13 Examine the imagery that surrounds Mrs Ramsay,
and comment on the total effect and impression.

14 What different kinds of humour are shown in the
book and for what purposes are they used?

15 Show how the book reflects the passing of time and
its effects; the tragedies and losses of life.

16 Mr and Mrs Ramsay have contrasting attitudes to
life. Discuss these contrasts and show what relation
they have to the meaning of the book as a whole.

17 Virginia Woolf writes only about a narrow range of
people: the intellectual, intelligent and artistic middle
class. Do you find this limiting and unlike real life – as
some critics do – or acceptable for the themes with
which she is dealing?

18 The characters in *To the Lighthouse* have been
criticized for being too symbolic and not sufficiently
individual. How far would you agree with this?

19 Show how Virginia Woolf's conception of 'real' life
was that of an inner awareness, of a spiritual fulfilment
that is essentially solitary and individual.

20 Discuss the significance of the structure of the book
in relation to the themes of time and the pattern of
life.

21 Discuss the meaning of Lily's picture and what
relation it has to past events, the Ramsays and herself.

22 Mrs Ramsay is only alive in the first part of the

book. Show how powerful her influence is there, and what part she still has to play in the second and third sections.

23 Discuss the importance of the dinner party to the meaning and themes of the book as a whole.

24 'The great revelation had never come. The great revelation perhaps never did come'. How far does this statement reflect the theme of the whole book?

Suggested notes for essay answer to question 1

Define the word '*elegy*' – make sure you are accurate – perhaps name one or two to demonstrate this (Gray's *Elegy...*) – show how the word could be applied to the novel – then brief definition of conventional novel (time sequence, beginning to end, etc.).

Consider the *deaths* in the novel – Mrs Ramsay's the most important – but think too of the passage of time – other deaths – the war – the elegiac nature of some of the prose – Lily's picture – the lighthouse itself.

Pay particular attention to the *movements of the consciousness* – the past always being present in the present – selective memory – connections and associations – other characters – shifts in narrative perspective through them, etc.

Now look at the *conventional novel* – beginning and end – generally a fixed narrative viewpoint – outside characters – action – say in what ways there is difference in this novel (everyday life – take the dinner party and show how this is differently presented to other comparable situations).

Now assert the case for *elegy* – decide whether you agree completely or have reservations – reasons for either – give instances from text which support your views – indicate as you do Virginia Woolf's main techniques.

Conclusion – reinforce your own judgement by citing instances not yet given of (a) the elegiac content (look particularly at Part 3) and (b) the main differences which place this work beyond the conventional novel – then, finally, argue *very briefly* for/against the title – possibility of another title.

Further reading

Other Works by Virginia Woolf and particularly
Mrs Dalloway
The Waves
Orlando
The Common Reader
Virginia Woolf: Her Art as a Novelist, Joan Bennett (Cambridge University Press)
To the Lighthouse, ed. Morris Beja (Macmillan Casebook Series)
Bloomsbury, Quentin Bell (Futura)
Virginia Woolf 1882–1912, Quentin Bell (Paladin)
Virginia Woolf 1912–1941, Quentin Bell (Paladin)
Downhill all the Way: Autobiography of the Years 1919–39, Leonard Woolf (Hogarth Press)

Brodie's Notes

TITLES IN THE SERIES

George Bernard Shaw	**Pygmalion**
Alan Sillitoe	**Selected Fiction**
John Steinbeck	**Of Mice and Men** and **The Pearl**
Alice Walker	**The Color Purple**

ENGLISH COURSEWORK BOOKS

Terri Apter	**Women and Society**
Kevin Dowling	**Drama and Poetry**
Philip Gooden	**Conflict**
Philip Gooden	**Science Fiction**
Margaret K. Gray	**Modern Drama**
Graham Handley	**Modern Poetry**
Graham Handley	**Prose**
Graham Handley	**Childhood and Adolescence**
R. J. Sims	**The Short Story**